UNDERSTANDING WHAT IT MEANS TO BE
BORN AGAIN
AND THINGS PERTAINING TO BEING BORN AGAIN

BY MIKE RECH

TRILOGY
A WHOLLY OWNED SUBSIDIARY OF **TBN**
PROFESSIONAL PUBLISHING MEETS POWERFUL PROMOTION

Trilogy Christian Publishers

A Wholly Owned Subsidiary of Trinity Broadcasting Network

2442 Michelle Drive

Tustin, CA 92780

Copyright © 2024 by Mike Rech

Scripture quotations marked AMP are taken from the Amplified Bible, Classic Edition. Copyright © 1954, 1958, 1962, 1964, 1965, 1987 by The Lockman Foundation. Used by permission. Scripture quotations marked ESV are taken from the ESV® Bible (The Holy Bible, English Standard Version®), copyright © 2001 by Crossway Bibles, a publishing ministry of Good News Publishers. Used by permission. All rights reserved. Scripture quotations marked NIV are taken from the Holy Bible, New International Version®, NIV®. Copyright © 1973, 1978, 1984, 2011 by Biblica, Inc.TM Used by permission of Zondervan. All rights reserved worldwide. www.zondervan.com. The "NIV" and "New International Version" are trademarks registered in the United States Patent and Trademark Office by Biblica, Inc.TM Scripture quotations marked NLT are taken from the Holy Bible, New Living Translation, copyright © 1996, 2004, 2015 by Tyndale House Foundation. Used by permission of Tyndale House Publishers, Inc., Carol Stream, Illinois 60188. All rights reserved. Scripture quotations marked KJV are taken from the King James Version of the Bible. Public domain.

All rights reserved, including the right to reproduce this book or portions thereof in any form whatsoever.

For information, address Trilogy Christian Publishing

Rights Department, 2442 Michelle Drive, Tustin, Ca 92780.

Trilogy Christian Publishing/ TBN and colophon are trademarks of Trinity Broadcasting Network.

For information about special discounts for bulk purchases, please contact Trilogy Christian Publishing.

Trilogy Disclaimer: The views and content expressed in this book are those of the author and may not necessarily reflect the views and doctrine of Trilogy Christian Publishing or the Trinity Broadcasting Network.

10 9 8 7 6 5 4 3 2 1

Library of Congress Cataloging-in-Publication Data is available.

ISBN 979-8-89333-193-6

ISBN 979-8-89333-194-3 (ebook)

Acknowledgment

I want to give a special thanks to three people for helping me write this book. My wife, Susan Rech, did proofreading to help me not have run-on sentences.

Pastor Donna Rounds did proofreading and asked me questions when something she felt was not right. She made suggestions on certain subjects of what I wrote.

Thanks to Pastor Ruben Ceballos for giving me permission to put his study outline on how to spiritually study the Bible. He also gave me permission to put in this book from a series of sermons that he did who Jesus is from each book in the Bible.

Table of Contents

Introduction 7

Chapter 1. My Testimony and What Caused Me to Change 11

Chapter 2. What Is the Bible? 26

Chapter 3. Concepts and Beliefs of the Bible 43

Chapter 4. The Love of God and Jesus for You 64

Chapter 5. What Happened to Jesus' Body While His Spirit Was in Hell, and What Happened When He Rose from the Dead? 100

Chapter 6. Why Did Jesus Have to Suffer, And What It Means to Be Born Again 116

Chapter 7. What Water Baptism Really Is 140

Chapter 8. Where Do Babies and Little Children Go When They Die? 157

Chapter 9. The Holy Spirit Dwelling in You 163

Chapter 10. Repenting Is a Part of Loving God 168

Chapter 11. What Is Sin? 182

Chapter 12. A New Creature in Christ 191

Chapter 13. What Did Jesus Save Us From? 209

Chapter 14. Being a Doer of the Word and Being Holy . . 220

Chapter 15. Jesus Is Our Advocate and Mediator 228

Chapter 16. Did Jesus Have Brothers and Sisters? 238

Chapter 17. When Is a Picture or Statue a
    Graven Image or Idol? 248

Chapter 18. The Importance of Worshipping
    God and Being on Time 256

Chapter 19. What Does God Say about Judging Others? . 275

Chapter 20. The Three Being One God (the Trinity) . . . 280

Chapter 21. A Short Review and Closing 291

Chapter 22. Guidelines to Studying the Bible
    by Pastor Ruben Ceballos 296

Study Guide and Tools by Pastor Ruben Ceballos 299

What Jesus Is from Genesis to Revelation by
Pastor Ruben Ceballos 301

When Were the Books of the Bible Written?. 305

Introduction

This book is not just for Christians but for non-Christians as well. The purpose of this book is to help people fully understand what it means to be born again according to the Bible, to get people saved, and to help strengthen Christians who are weak in their Christian walk to become strong.

To those who have never read the Bible and know little about the Bible, you will want to read this book. You will be reading things about the Bible that you have never read before and reading verses that you did not know were in the Bible. There are things about the Bible and verses in the Bible that some religions will not tell you. Yes, you may have been told about these subjects, but you were never told of the verses on these subjects that are in the Bible in this book. You have never been told all of what the Bible says on these subjects.

First, a look at what changed me from not wanting anything to do with God to now not wanting to live without Him. Read about my dramatic life experience of how I faced death and lived to tell about it.

We will look a little at what the Bible is and what it is to us. Followed by an in-depth look at how much God really loves you and how much you really mean to God. After that, we will look at salvation and what it means. What does the term "born again" mean? Why be born again? Who is going to heaven, and who is not going to heaven? Why did Jesus Christ have to die on the cross? What does God's Word, the Bible, say about these things?

We are going to see what God says about water baptism, babies, little children, and about the Holy Spirit dwelling in you. We will also look at some of the things God says about worshipping Him. We will see who Jesus Christ is. We will also look at some guidelines for studying the Bible and dates of when the books of the Bible were written.

Do you believe in God? Do you believe in heaven and hell? Do you want to know what God says in the Bible about you, if you are going to heaven or not? If your answers are yes to these questions, and you want to know if you are going to heaven, then this is the book for you!

I will be using the King James Version (KJV), the Amplified Bible version (AMP), the English Standard Version (ESV), and/or the New International Version (NIV) of the Bible. There will be a few verses from the New Living Translation (NLT). The New Living Translation is not the Living Bible. The reasons for using these versions of the Bible are:

1. The King James Version is the most widely used Bible by Christians.

2. The Amplified Bible explains the meaning of each verse by using a lot of added descriptive words in each verse of the Bible. It brings out a much fuller meaning of each verse in the Bible.

3. The New Living Translation, the English Standard Version, and the New International Version are written in the English we speak today.

There are a few times when I put at least two or three versions of the Bible to make a point and to better understand what the verse is saying. Reading more than one version of the Bible gives us a better understanding of the doctrinal beliefs of the Bible. Some Bibles state verses better than other Bibles. In reading the preface of the New International Version Bible and the English Standard Version Bible it says they are translated from Hebrew, Aramaic, and Greek texts. Bible publishers only allow a certain percentage of quotations to be used in a book, so I am limited to how many verses I can write in this book.

The terms the Bible, God's Word, and the Word are synonymous and will be used interchangeably.

I do not claim to know all the answers, but with the answers I do know, God is showing me what to say and write in this book.

Warning! There are doctrinal facts of what to believe from the Bible in this book that may/or will offend someone's religious beliefs. My intention is not to offend, but I am showing you from the Bible what God says about the things we are to believe. You will have to decide for yourself if you are going to continue to believe the religious doctrine you have been taught or the Bible. Which is correct, your religion or the Bible? Who is man to say their religion is correct and the Bible is wrong? Do you want to believe man-made beliefs or God? To believe God is to believe the Bible, not man. Remember, I am only pointing out what the Bible is saying about the doctrinal beliefs that you should have. Read and study it for yourself to see that the Bible is correct and not man/or religion. Remember, God and Jesus did not half-step, water down, or go easy on people as a whole when they were doing things wrong. Needless to say, God is not letting me half-step in this book. Your toes may be stepped on by God and His Bible. One cannot say their beliefs are right if they do not read and study the Bible.

Part of being born again is knowing:

- Jesus Christ as your personal Savior and following Him.
- What the correct beliefs are and are not regarding or concerning God and the Bible.
- Who Jesus is, what He did, and why He did it.
- What the Bible is.
- What God wants us to do and believe.
- What the will of God is.

In John 3:3, 5, Jesus said, we cannot see the kingdom of God nor enter it unless we are born again. Then, in verse 7, He said that we must be born again. My intent is to help you understand what it means to be born again according to the Bible and to help you know God and Jesus through simple instructions. We will look at these verses and other verses in a way that most people do not look at them.

After reading this book, you will completely understand what the term "born again" means and why Jesus said, "We must be born again."

CHAPTER 1:

MY TESTIMONY AND WHAT CAUSED ME TO CHANGE

When I was nine, I completed my catechism. I don't remember what I was taught, but I realized at that time that I was not going to heaven. Even though I did not know anything about the Bible or had ever read the Bible, I knew I was going to hell, and because of that, I decided to quit going to church. I used the excuse that I got sick when they would burn the incense just before communion, which sometimes did make me sick. This is what I told my mom, and she was okay with it. I figured—what's the sense of going to church for one hour and making like I was holy when I knew that when I left the church, I would do the things that God would not want me to do? That is why I quit going to church. Whenever I sinned, I figured I might as well go all the way with whatever it was because I was going to hell and going to pay for it anyway. That is how I grew up.

When I was nineteen, I joined the Marine Corps, and I went to Vietnam. When I was in Vietnam, there were a couple of times that if you look at the situation in the natural, I should have been dead. One of the times, the point man got hit by a booby trap, and then we were fired upon. Shortly after it was over, we secured the area. During the firefight, I quickly jumped into a hole in the ground, which seemed to cover my whole body. All that was sticking out, so I thought, was my head and my rifle while I was shooting at the enemy.

When it was all over, I went back to that hole in the ground, and tried to get back into it, and I could only get the lower half of my body in it. There was no protection around that hole. By all means, the enemy should have been able to kill me, but they didn't. Another time, a buddy and I were on a lookout point. When our trip flares lit, we saw the movement in the brush and started to open fire. Following the movement, we also called for backup.

Blooper is another name we use for a grenade launcher. A man with a blooper came up from behind us and was shooting grenades at the enemy over our heads. He yelled, "Short round! Hit the deck!"

Standing with my rifle in my hands, before I could drop down, the grenade blew up within eight feet in front of me. Shrapnel hit the helmet of the guy directly behind me. He yelled out to me, asking if I was okay. I yelled out, "Yes!" and asked why, and that's when he told me that shrapnel had hit his helmet. Again, I didn't get a single scratch from the grenade. I was between the man and the grenade and was much closer to the grenade, yet I did not get a single scratch.

When I got home from Vietnam, my mom told me that she prayed every night for God to bring me home safely and in one piece. I believe that it was her prayers and her unwavering faith in God that brought me home in one piece, safe and sound. That is why God's angels protected me.

Before I got saved, I smoked up to a pack and a half a day and drank my whole weekends through. I drank so much that my friends nicknamed me "wino." I had a filthy mouth and could not say one complete sentence without swearing. I've done a lot of other sinful things, but I'd rather not go into any detail about them.

I spent the last ten months of my service at Camp Pendleton, California. Three months before I was to get out, I decided I wanted to learn more about my religion and beliefs. I also decided to travel home by car, not by plane. I received my Honorable Discharge on February 8, 1972. On the 9th, I started driving home to Milwaukee, Wisconsin. Since it was the middle of winter, I decided to take the southern route, which was I-20 from California to Dallas, Texas. From there, I was going to angle up to Wisconsin. That way, I would be halfway home before I would hit bad weather. I was traveling at night time and sleeping during the day, because it was warmer during the day.

On February 11, 1972, I got this very scary feeling from head to toe. I felt like I was in someone else's body. I was so scared that I started to pray. I felt Our Father and Hail Mary were not going to do it. Those were the only two prayers that I knew.

I said, "God, I do not know what is going to happen to me. I just know something terrible is going to happen. I ask that whatever it is, You heal me back to normal. I ask that I would not be disfigured in any way, that I don't lose any parts of my body, and that I have no scars. I ask that I can walk and talk and do everything just like before my accident. I also ask that no one else gets badly hurt but me. Amen."

As soon as I finished my prayer, my accident began to happen. I was thirteen miles out of Big Spring, Texas, on I-20 in the desert. It was about 1 a.m. It was cloudy and so dark you could not see your hand in front of your face. What I didn't know was that I was traveling from a good-weather area to a bad-weather area. It had rained, stopped, and then froze to black ice. I was on a curb that was banked to my left. The rear end of my car came to my left. I was so scared that I think I panicked and floored it instead of pumping the brakes because I am sure when I looked at my speedometer, it said 45 mph. The police report said I was doing 60 mph. I tried to straighten the car out, and it went to my right. I tried to straighten it out again, and my car went back to my left, and I made three full spins into the oncoming traffic. As I came out of my third spin, I hit another car head-on. When I saw the other car, my only thought was, *I'm dead.* After hitting the other car, my car bounced back into the mid-strip.

Not knowing how long I was sitting there, I found myself frozen to the steering wheel and the brakes. I started to check myself out to see if I was okay. It was so dark out that all I could see was the dome light from the other car. When I got out of my car to run and see how the other people in the other car were, I fell into a squatting position, and that's how I ran to the other car. When I got to their car, I was finally able to stand upright. The father of the family was sitting on the street and holding onto the inside handle of the car door. I figured his nerves were shot like mine because he was just sitting there, staring straight ahead.

His wife was yelling, "My legs! My legs!" so I checked to see if there was any blood. I remembered my first aid training and how to stop limbs from bleeding, and figured that if I saw blood, I could stop the bleeding—but there wasn't any blood. I looked at the kids in the back seat, and they were just crying from the fear of it all.

Then, I saw a semi coming straight for their car. I ran between the car and the semi and flagged him down, and he went between the two cars. A second semi came along, and I tried to flag him down. Pretty soon, he got so close that I had to turn and run towards the car and then tried to flag him down again.

Just then, the mother yelled, "Hurry up, kids, get out of the car!"

I felt it was my fault that they were there, so I kept trying to flag the truck down to give the family time to run to safety. When the driver finally took action, it was too late for me to run from him. He started jack-knifing to my right. I got a glimpse of the rail to my left before his headlights weren't on it anymore. Not knowing that I had spun onto an overpass, I took a flying leap over the rail, thinking the ground on the other side was the same level as what I was standing on.

Once I jumped over, everything turned pitch black again. All I could hear was the sound of the semi hitting the car, the metal smashing, and the glass breaking. When it got silent, I realized that I hadn't touched the ground yet. I thought, *Gee, I didn't touch ground yet. I wonder how far.* Just then, I hit the ground, my back facing the ground, and my arms, legs, and head were all facing upward, all bunched together. I landed on a hump in the ground next to the railroad tracks that went underneath the overpass. After I hit the ground, I had the wind knocked out of me, and I was in so much pain in my back that I started to roll around all over, gasping for air and trying to find some relief from the pain.

At that point, I saw a light shining from above, and it went by me twice.

Then I heard somebody say, "I can't find him."

So, I started to groan as loud as I could. I remembered my military training that if you make noise at night, the enemy will find you. I kept up the groaning until they found me.

Then, I heard someone say, "Now, how do we get to him? We have only one flashlight."

I kept groaning. When they got to me, I laid straight, and I felt a bunch of hands go underneath me. Then, they picked me up and put me on a stretcher. It felt like they carried me downhill first and then uphill back to the road. I was asked if I wanted to go to a VA Hospital, and I groaned a yes for it. While I was being carried to the ambulance, I kept asking, with difficulty, if the family of the other car was okay until somebody said yes. When I arrived at my room at the hospital, I passed out and went into a coma for four and a half days.

From my fall, I received two fractures in my spine and had internal bruises throughout my back. Even though it was four and a half days later, I still had a hard time breathing. The newspaper said I fell twenty-five feet, and the police report said that I fell approximately sixty feet. I have worked inside of a railroad car. It is twenty-five feet from the floor to the ceiling. I know I fell more than twenty-five feet. The family of the car that I hit ran to safety before the semi hit their car.

The semi driver did not get hurt either. God had answered my prayer of faith completely. I was the only one that got badly hurt. The parents had minor bruises, but the children and truck driver did not get physically hurt at all. God healed my body completely. I can walk, talk, and do everything just like before my accident.

When I woke up, I saw some IVs in me, and I thought it was the next day after my accident. As soon as the nurses saw I was awake, they treated me for shock. When I realized that it was the fifth day after my accident, my mind was overwhelmed. I could not believe that I had been out for four and a half days. It really was mind-boggling, but thanks to the nurses knowing what to do, I did not go into shock. The nurses told me to stay lying straight on my back, but they wouldn't tell me why. I had to lay that way for three weeks until they got the body cast on me. As much pain as I was in, it was not easy.

The day before I left the hospital to come home, one of the nurses told me that the slightest wrong movement before they got the body cast on me could have paralyzed me for life. The night of my accident, I rolled around like crazy, not knowing my fractures could have cut my spinal cord and paralyzed me for life. Even at that point, God was watching over me and protecting me.

One week after I was in the VA Hospital, a man named Dick Bartlett came up to see me. He introduced himself and said he had read about my accident in the newspaper. He said that the other day, when he looked at the article again, God told him to come and see me.

When he said that, I thought, *Yeah, right, God's talking to you.*

Dick asked me if I needed any help. I did, but I didn't answer him right away.

That night, I asked a nurse if she knew him, and she said yes. She told me he visits the men and helps them when he can. I did need help. I was hauled off to the hospital, and my car and stuff were hauled off to the junkyard after the accident. Dick got my stuff for me.

After three weeks of visitation, Dick asked me if I was born again. I tried to figure out how I could get back into my mother's womb again.

I thought, *There's no way I can do that. Is this guy nuts?* Then I said, "No, I am not born again."

Then, Dick told me how to be born again. He told me by doing this, I would go to heaven. He also told me I would have to repent and turn away from my sinful ways. The first thing I thought about was all the sins that I had committed, like the ones I mentioned earlier. I thought that because of my filthy mouth, I would not be able to talk. I also thought I would miss all the sinful things that I did. But I wanted so much to go to heaven and not go to hell that I decided to accept Jesus Christ as my personal Savior. I decided to forget or turn away from my sinful ways, and if life got too boring, I'd just go back to them. I prayed a prayer like this one:

Dear God, I believe with all my heart that Jesus died for me. That You, God, have raised Him from the dead, and that Jesus is Lord. I repent of my sins and ask You, Jesus, for forgiveness of all my sins. I accept Your forgiveness and ask You, Jesus, to come into my heart. I accept You as my personal Savior. I commit and give my life to You. Please fill me now with the Holy Spirit. I thank You, Jesus, for saving me. In Jesus' name, I pray. Amen.

After I prayed this prayer, God started to change me. I found out I could still have fun in life without all the sinful things that I used to do. Life still has its ups and downs, but now I can go through life with Jesus to help me. I did not change overnight, but over the days, months, and years, I sin less and less. Some things I was able to quit doing right away, and other things took a while. For example, it took me one year to get swearing out of my regular vocabulary and three more years to get it out of my system when I would get upset about something. I am not perfect. Because I am human, I still, at times, fall to temptation, but I strive to continue to try not to sin; this is something that nobody can do without God, Jesus, and the Holy Spirit in their lives.

When I was ready to come home to Milwaukee, Wisconsin, Dick told me the name and address of a church to go to. He gave me the name of the pastor, and said to go there. Dick told me that I would grow in the Lord and get to know the pastor and people at that church. When I got home, I did not go to the church.

Three months later, Dick sent a letter to the church and asked how I was doing there. The church secretary read the letter and thought, *Who is this guy by the name of Michael Rech?* So, she wrote a letter back to him and said that they did not know who I was.

Once a year, this church has an international convention in Anderson, Indiana, and Dick had planned to go to the convention. After the convention, he came the rest of the way up to Milwaukee, Wisconsin. He arrived on Monday and stayed with us for the week, and we went to church on Sunday. Talk about follow-up! Dick came all the way from Big Spring, Texas, just to take me to church. I have been with the Lord ever since then. Even though I know it does not make up for the tragedy that the family went through, I give my deepest apology to the family of the car that I hit. I am sorry.

Since then, I have studied the Bible and sat under teachings about the Bible for over thirty-six years. I feel and believe that God has given me enough knowledge to know what I am talking about in being born again and the other subjects in this book.

As you will see, the Bible is very clear on what it means to be saved. The Bible is also very clear on all the other subjects that God wants me to talk about in this book.

During and/or before the 1970s, you did not hear very much of the term born again. Most people did not know the term or had never heard of the term. The term born again has always been in the Bible. A lot of people today have heard of the term but are not fully informed of what the term means, according to the Bible.

For legal reasons, I blotted out the names of the other people in the newspaper article. The newspaper article has the wrong car doing the spinning. The following is a newspaper article about my accident, a part of the police report stating that I fell approximately sixty feet, three pictures of the car I was in, and a picture of the overpass that I jumped off of, plus a picture of me in my body cast.

Chapter 1: My Testimony and What Caused Me to Change

EAST OF COAHOMA

Glaze Causes 2 Accidents On Overpass

Ice on the Texas and Pacific Railroad overpass east of Coahoma is believed to have caused two separate accidents shortly before 1 a.m. today which resulted in three persons, one listed in serious condition, being taken to two Big Spring hospitals.

Michael J. Rech, 21, Milwaukee, Wis., is in serious condition at Veterans Administration Hospital where he is being examined for spinal and possible internal injuries, which he received as a result of a fall from the bridge, not of the collision.

Rech was in the east bound lane of IS 20 when his car hit the icy bridge, and he lost control. His vehicle crossed the median and was involved in a head-on collision in the westbound lane with a car driven by ███████, 35, ██████ ██. ██████ and his wife, ████, 29, are both listed in satisfactory condition at Medical Center Memorial Hospital.

████████ car spun three times after impact and came to rest in the median, partially blocking the inside east and west bound lanes.

Rech, ████████, his wife, and their two children, ████, 11, and ████, 7, had reportedly exited their vehicles and stood in the one east bound lane that had not been blocked by the wreck. After impact, Rech's vehicle had continued west in the west bound lane, and had struck the guard rail approximately 150 feet away from point of impact.

At this point, a truck-tractor and trailer rig belonging to ██████ Transport, ██████ and driven by ██████ ██ ████, 25, Sweetwater, topped the bridge heading east.

████ told officers that the people were standing in the only clear lane for east bound traffic, and he swerved into the ██████ vehicle in the median. ████ truck came to a stop, entangled with the car, and his trailer came to rest against the east bound lane guardrail. ████ was not injured.

The ██████ and their children ran a short distance down the highway to get out of the way of the truck. Rech, on seeing the truck approach, leaped the guardrail and took a 25-foot fall to the ground below the bridge.

The accidents occurred at 12:50 a.m. and 12:51 a.m., and it was 2:30 a.m. before Texas Highway Patrol, deputy sheriffs and two wrecker units were able to clear the traffic lanes.

The trucker was able to continue on his way to Abilene, but the two cars were demolished.

Alert Ambulance units took the injured to the hospitals, and the two ██████ children were later picked up at the hospital by relatives from Odessa whom the family had been going to visit.

Investigating officers were Texas Highway Patrolmen ██████ and ██████ ██████, assisted by Deputy Sheriffs ██████ ██████ and ██████.

UNIT NO. 1		VEHICLE REMOVED TO	Driven from scene						
DAMAGE RATING	FL-3	BY	By operator						

SEAT POSITION	OCCUPANTS NAMES Show Last Name First	ADDRESS	HEAD REST	STRAP USED	BELT USED	AGE	SEX	INJURY CODE
Front Left	Driver, See Front							
Front Center								
Front Right								
Rear Left								
Rear Center								
Rear Right								

UNIT NO. 2 (Complete only if Unit No. 2 was a motor vehicle.)		VEHICLE REMOVED TO	Independent Wrecking Yard Big Spring						
DAMAGE RATING	BL-4	BY	Independent Wrecker Big Spring (P)						

SEAT POSITION	OCCUPANTS NAMES Show Last Name First	ADDRESS	HEAD REST	STRAP USED	BELT USED	AGE	SEX	INJURY CODE
Front Left	Driver, See Front							
Front Center								
Front Right								
Rear Left								
Rear Center								
Rear Right								

COMPLETE IF CASUALTIES NOT IN MOTOR VEHICLE

PEDESTRIAN, BICYCLIST, ETC. Show Last Name First	CASUALTY NAME	CASUALTY ADDRESS	AGE	SEX	INJURY CODE

DISPOSITION OF KILLED AND INJURED

ITEM NUMBERS	TAKEN TO	BY

IF AMBULANCE USED SHOW	Time Ambulance Driver Notified	Time arrived at Scene	Number of Ambulance Attendants incl. Driver
		M _____ M	

.....CONTINUANCE OF **DESCRIBE WHAT HAPPENED** SECTION FROM THE FRONT.....

However, the occupants of the units which were previously wrecked were standing in the roadway. The driver of Unit #1 elected to collide with Unit #2 instead of with the pedestrians on the roadway. The front left of Unit #1 struck the back left of Unit #2. The pedestrians saw the Unit #1 approaching and were attempting to get out of its path. Four of the pedestrians ran down the roadway to the east. One of the pedestrians thought the bridge on which they were standing was on a small hill. He then jumped over the side of the bridge and was critically injured when he fell approximately 60 feet. Unit #1 came to rest blocking both eastbound lanes of traffic still connected to Unit #2. Unit #2 came to rest facing west in the eastbound lane.

CHAPTER 1: MY TESTIMONY AND WHAT CAUSED ME TO CHANGE

This was the car I drove.

The overpass.

Me in my body cast.

The reason there is a hole in my body cast is that after a while, I was feeling better and eating better, and one day, I had trouble breathing because of the weight gain, and the body cast didn't expand. So they cut a hole in the cast so I could breathe.

CHAPTER 2:

WHAT IS THE BIBLE?

One note for those who feel they cannot understand the Bible. The Bible is easier to understand when you read another English translation other than the King James Version. The basic biblical beliefs in the Bible are not hard to understand. As you will see as I explain them in this book. What is hard to understand is the English language from the sixteenth century that the King James Version is written in. The King James Version is not the only accurate English translation of the Bible.

The Bible is not man's written word.

Second Timothy 3:16:

King James Version (KJV), "[16] All scripture is given by inspiration of God, and is profitable for doctrine, for reproof, for correction, for instruction in righteousness."

Amplified Bible (AMP), "[16] Every Scripture is God-breathed (given by His inspiration) and profitable for instruction, for reproof and conviction of sin, for correction of error and discipline in obedience, [and] for training in righteousness (in holy living, in conformity to God's will in thought, purpose, and action.)"

English Standard Version (ESV), "[16] All Scripture is breathed out by God and profitable for teaching, for reproof, for correction, and for the training in righteousness."

New International Version (NIV), "[16] All Scripture is God-breathed and is useful for teaching, rebuking, correcting and training in righteousness."

This verse says a lot, but what I want to point out is that *all* Scripture is inspired by God. God gave and told man what to write in the Bible. Not only did God give the Scriptures to man, but God inspired man to write the Bible. It is God's words, not man's.

Second Peter 1:20–21:

(KJV), [20] "Knowing this first, that no prophecy of the Scripture is of any private interpretation.

[21] For the prophecy came not in old time by the will of man: but holy men of God spoke as they were moved by the Holy Ghost."

(AMP), [20] "[Yet] first [you must] understand this, that no prophecy of Scripture is [a matter] of any personal or private or special interpretation (loosening, solving).

[21] For no prophecy ever originated because some man willed it [to do so—it never came by human impulse], but men spoke from God who were borne along (moved and impelled) by the Holy Spirit."

(NIV), [20] "Above all, you must understand that no prophecy of Scripture came about by the prophet's own interpretation of things.

[21] For prophecy never had its origin in the human will, but prophets, though human, spoke from God as they were carried along by the Holy Spirit."

As we read in the Scriptures themselves, man was moved and inspired by God and the Holy Spirit. Man wrote what the Holy Spirit told him to write. The Bible, the Word of God, was given to us by God. God used men to write the Bible. Man did not come up with the Bible on his own, nor did he come up with the great wisdom that is in the Bible.

What is the Bible? The Bible is God's Word and will for all men, for every man, woman, and child, for the whole world. The Old Testament was originally written in Hebrew, and a small portion of it was written in Aramaic. It is the old covenant that God had with man, but a lot of it still applies to us today. The New Testament was originally written in Greek and is God's new covenant and will for us today. The New Testament is also the fulfillment of the Old Testament. There are sixty-six books in the Bible: thirty-nine in the Old Testament and twenty-seven in the New Testament.

Note: When the Bible was originally written, it did not have paragraphs, chapters, or verse numbers in it. They were put in the Bible by the scholars so we can find where everything is in the Bible. This makes it a lot easier to read and study the Bible.

The books in the Bible were not all written in the same time period. After the first five books were written, hundreds of years went by before any of the other books were written.

There were also long periods of time between the other books. The amazing part about this is that all the books in the Bible are in agreement with each other. They back each other on doctrinal beliefs.

Biblical canonizing is determining what books are to be biblical books that are spiritually inspired by God. The Jews are God's chosen people, and the Jewish rabbis and scholars kept the books called the Torah, the Law and the prophets. It is said that Jesus never quoted anything from books that are not in the Old Testament.

There is so much to say on the canonization of the Old Testament that I would have to write over a few chapters to totally explain it right, which I don't feel led to do. There is no exact time recorded of when the canonizing of the Old Testament was completed. Scholars today believe the Old Testament was canonized by the end of the fifth century.

Here is a very short summary of the canonizing of the New Testament. The New Testament was canonized in 393 AD by the Council of Hippo and at a later time in 397 AD by the Council of Carthage with certain requirements, and both councils affirmed the same twenty-seven books as the authoritative books for the New Testament.

Note: The writings of the New Testament were started ten to thirteen years after Jesus died and were finished between sixty-two and sixty-five years after Jesus died. From 44 AD to 96 AD, the whole New Testament was written in a time period of only fifty-two years.

From different resources, here are three sets of the requirements said to have been used by the councils to determine if the scriptures of the books were inspired by the Holy Spirit or not.

Set one.

1. Was the author an apostle, or have a close connection with an apostle?
2. Is the book being accepted by the body of Christ at large?
3. Did the book contain consistency of doctrine and orthodox teaching?
4. Did the book bear evidence of high moral and spiritual values that would reflect a work of the Holy Spirit?

Set two.

1. Does the book contain apostolic authority? Meaning was the author an apostle or a direct associate (eye-witness) with an apostle?
2. Is the book continuously used and accepted by the Christian community at large?
3. Is the book consistent with orthodox teaching and doctrine?

Set three.

1. Was it written by one of Jesus' disciples—someone who was an eyewitness to Jesus' ministry (such as Peter) or someone who interviewed eyewitnesses (such as Luke)?

2. Was it written in the first century AD? Meaning, books were not included if they were written long after the events of Jesus' life and the first decades of the church.

3. Was it consistent with the other portions of Scripture known to be valid? Meaning, the book could not contradict another element of Scripture that was trusted.

Those requirements are excellent guidelines for making sure we have accurate accounts of the truth of what God wanted us to have in His Bible. Christianity has survived for over 2000 years on the Bible. Therefore, there is no need for more books to be added to the Bible and no need to change the doctrinal beliefs of the Bible.

It is also said after a few decades of debate, these councils largely settled on which books should be included in the Bible. In the end, it was God who decided what books belonged in the biblical canonization of the Bible. God inspired man to write the Bible; surly, God inspired man to canonize the Bible.

The main reason for canonizing the books to be in the Bible was so the common Christians would know and would not have to decide which writings or books were to be accepted as the true Word of God. It was done to make sure that Christians would not be led astray in believing and practicing doctrinal beliefs that were not taught by Jesus and His disciples. Because there are writings and books that contradict, teach, and promote beliefs that were not taught by Jesus and His disciples.

Yet man has learned how to take scriptures out of context from the Bible and get people to religiously believe the wrong things. Man still teaches and promotes religious things from historical books and gospels that are not inspired by God. Man believes things from historical books that contradict the Bible because, today, man does not accept and/or read the entire Bible for himself.

For those who do not know much about the Bible, I want to give you a little information about the Bibles of the verses that I am using in this book. It is good to know something about the English translations that you will be reading.

The King James Version was not the first English translation of the Bible. Here are some of the Bibles that were translated into English before the King James Bible.

Great Bible in 1539, Geneva Bible in 1560, Bishops Bible in 1568, the New Testament of the Douay-Rheims Bible in 1582, and in 1609–1610, the Old Testament of the Douay-Rheims Bible. Note: the Douay-Rheims Bible is a Roman Catholic version of the Bible.

King James despised the popular household Geneva Bible of his time because he was annoyed by the marginal notes in that Bible—for the notes allowed disobedience to tyrannical kings. The notes comprised close to 300,000 words, almost one-third of the length of the Bible. The marginal notes were in the Geneva Bible for a better understanding of the scriptures. The main reason why King James wanted and ordered a new English translation was to get rid of the marginal notes. He implied the new translation would be a more accurate Bible, hoping it would become the popular household Bible amongst the common people. Today, the King James Version is over 400 years old, and it is popular just like the king wanted it to be.

The King James Version was translated into the English language from Latin by forty-seven scholars from the Church of England. They started in 1604 and completed it in 1611. When the scholars were done, they named the Bible after King James, which is now known as the King James Version. The King James Version has been revised several times since 1611. One of the reasons why is that the meaning of over 300 words in the English language has changed.

The Amplified Bible was completed in 1965. To me, its purpose is to better understand the Bible by using a lot more descriptive words in each verse.

It was taught that the Old Testament was originally written in Hebrew. Today, there are scholars who say a small portion of the Old Testament was written in Arabic, and there are scholars who still say it was all written in Hebrew only. I am not going to argue the point one way or another. My point is the Bible is from God.

The New International Version was started in 1965 and was first copyrighted in 1973. Over a hundred scholars worked hard going directly to the best available Hebrew, Arabic, and Greek manuscripts or texts. A large number of church leaders from many different denominations participated in the translation. The scholars were biblical scholars from seminaries, universities, and colleges. I think the reason why many different denominations and biblical scholars translated this Bible together was so no one denomination would have their own interpretation of the verses in the Bible. They wanted to be as accurate as possible, to have the doctrine of God in the Bible and not the doctrine of man.

The New Living Translation was started in 1986 and was completed and copyrighted in 1996. It was done by ninety translators. The Amplified Bible, The New Living Translation Bible, and The Living Bible are paraphrased Bibles, each done differently, which helps us to understand the Bible.

The English Standard Version Bible, like the NIV, was translated from Hebrew, Arabic, and Greek manuscripts or texts to keep an accurate interpretation of the Bible in English. The English Standard Version Bible was first published in 2001. It was translated by over fifty biblical experts, plus another fifty who made up an advisory council. This team came together from twelve countries, representing twenty different denominations.

This is for those who do not know what a red-letter Bible is. When a Bible is called a red-letter Bible that means all the words that Jesus said are written in red.

For those who have never read the Bible, the table of contents will tell you where each book is in the Bible. For example, when you see John 3:16, the name John is the book in the Bible. The number before the colon is the chapter, and the number after the colon is the verse in that chapter. The chapter number is usually a little bigger than the verse number in the Bible. This example will be repeated one more time later in this book.

The Bible is not a religion, religion's will, church's will, or man's will, but it is God's will and only God's will. This is why I have a lot of Bible verses in my book, to show you it is not just what I believe, but it is God's will. The Bible is our manual from God on how to live a Christian life. Just like a car has a manual on how to operate and run it, the Bible is God's manual and way for everyone to live their life. It is our manual to know what to believe and what not to believe. Reading the Bible helps you to know what God's will is for you. Again, God gave us the Bible, not man or a religion.

Numbers 23:19 (AMP)

¹⁹ God is not a man, that He should tell or act a lie, neither the son of man, that He should feel repentance or compunction [for what He has promised]. Has He said and shall He not do it? Or has He spoken and shall He not make it good?"

Titus 1:2 (AMP)

² [Resting] in the hope of eternal life, [life] which the ever truthful God Who cannot deceive promised before the world or the ages of time began.

First Corinthians 14:33 (AMP)

³³ For He [Who is the source of their prophesying] is not a God of confusion and disorder but of peace and order. As [is the practice] in all the churches of the saints (God's people).

The Bible is the truth. God will not and cannot lie. God is not a God of confusion or disorder but a God of peace of mind. If the Bible had contradictions in it, then God would have to be a God of confusion and disorder, which He is not. Therefore, there are no contradictions in the Bible, only our misinterpretations or misunderstanding of the Holy Scriptures. Remember 2 Timothy 3:16; this verse says that all Scripture (every single verse in the Bible) is God-breathed, inspired, and given by God, profitable for instruction, for reproof and conviction of sin, for correction of error, and discipline in obedience. For the training in righteousness in holy living, conforming to God's will in thought, purpose, and action.

> Second Timothy 3:17 (AMP)
>
> ¹⁷ So that the man of God may be complete and proficient, well fitted and thoroughly equipped for every good work.

God uses the Bible to prepare and equip His people to do every good work, not bad works or evil. He is the main author of the Bible, Who, at the right time, gave man each book and what to write about in it. Ecclesiastes 3:1 (paraphrased by the author), "For everything there is a season, and a time for every purpose under heaven."

In Titus 1:2, we are told that God cannot lie. With the verses that I have given you so far, I rest my case: God gave us His Word, the Bible, not man.

This is for those who know very little about the Bible. Notice even though we have many English versions or translations of the Bible that are worded differently, they are still in agreement with each other. They have the same books, the same Gospels, and the same doctrine, but again, just worded differently. There are many English translations not because God's Word has changed but because the meanings of the words in the English language keep changing.

The biblical scholars will revise the existing Bibles or make a new translation of the Bible as the meanings of the English words change. Here are three more reasons of maybe why we have different English versions or translations of the Bible today.

1. Everyone cannot understand the King James English language because we do not talk that way today.
2. The different English versions or translations of the Bible can help us to better understand the King James English.
3. Some English versions or translations of the Bible say certain verses better than others.

These three reasons are not the main reasons why we have so many different versions or translations of the Bible, but they are good ones for why we should read more than just one version or translation of the Bible.

In the following paragraph, I am stating facts about a certain religion, their beliefs, and their Bible.

There is one Bible that I know of that does not agree with some of the doctrines of the other English translations and/or with the Hebrew and Greek manuscripts: The New World Translation or The New World Translation of the Holy Scriptures. This Bible is not the same as the Bible. This Bible is used by the Jehovah's Witnesses, known as the Watchtower Society. According to their beliefs, Jesus was just a man called a god. Jesus is not God. There are other doctrines in their Bible that disagree with the Bible.

Oops! There is a second bible that I know of that does not agree with the other English Bibles and the Hebrew and Greek manuscripts. The meanings of certain verses have been changed to make the Bible gay-friendly. It is the Queen James Bible, published in 2012. All the verses that condemn homosexuality do not condemn homosexuality in it.

"Mike, when I read the Bible, I do not understand it." My guess is you are reading only the King James Version Bible. I suggest you get and read the Amplified Bible, the New International Version Bible, the English Standard Version, or all three. This will make it much easier to understand the Bible. The other Bibles will help you to understand the King James Version Bible.

"Mike, why do you say the King James Version Bible?" Because the full name of the King James Bible is the King James Version. For political reasons, at certain times, I have to use the full name of each Bible.

The King James Bible is not the only correct English translation of the Bible, as some think or are taught to believe. The New International Version Bible and the English Standard Version Bible are easier to understand than the King James Version Bible. The Amplified Bible is paraphrased with many added words to make the Bible easier to understand. By using these or other English Bibles it will help you to understand the King James Bible. Read and study the Bible of your choice.

Man-made beliefs may keep you out of heaven. Why? Because man-made beliefs do not line up with the Bible. Anybody in their right mind will not want to go to hell. The Bible says that those who are cast into the lake of fire will be tormented day and night forever and ever (Revelation 20:10, 15). The Bible is very clear on things and can be understood when you have the Holy Spirit in you.

Chapter 2: What Is the Bible?

There are those who say there are missing books of the Bible and that the Bible is not complete. The manuscripts of these missing books most likely have things in them that do not agree with and/or contradict the Bible. That is why these other books are not in the Bible. These so called missing books and manuscripts are not deemed as scriptures inspired by God and the Holy Spirit. They may have historical history in them, but when it comes to God, Jesus, or other spiritual matters, they are contradictory to the Bible. All the books in the Bible are in agreement with each other, and none of them have contradictions in them. There are no missing books of the Bible; the Bible is complete.

If, and I mean if, there are missing books of the Bible, are you saying that the forty-seven scholars from the Church of England are wrong? Are you saying that over a hundred biblical scholars from seminaries, universities, and colleges who went directly to the best available Hebrew, Arabic, and Greek manuscripts or texts are wrong? That a large number of church leaders from many different denominations that helped the over one hundred biblical scholars in translating the Bible are wrong? That over fifty biblical experts of one hundred more translators of the English Standard Version Bible are wrong? Are you saying that they all left some books out of the Bible? I don't think so!

They all had nothing to benefit themselves other than to be as accurate as possible. I do not believe that they all left books out of the Bible and are wrong. God is all-knowing and all-powerful. Do you think God would let man leave a book He wanted out of the Bible? I don't think so. Again, I say there are no missing books of the Bible; the Bible is complete.

One more thing…to say there are missing books in the Bible is to say that the Council of Hippo and the Council of Carthage did not know what they were doing when they canonized the Bible. To say, "Well, we are smarter now," would be wrong, too. For example, with all the modern technology we have today, we still cannot figure out exactly how the Egyptian pyramids were built.

Once again, the Bible is God's written Word. Given by God to man, and not given by man to man. It is "God-breathed, inspired, and given by God, profitable for instruction, for reproof and conviction of sin, for correction of error and discipline in obedience. For the training in righteousness in holy living, conforming to God's will in thought, purpose, and action." The Bible is not a religion, of a religion, or from a religion. It is from God and is the Word of God. Which do you believe is correct…man-made beliefs that are not in the Bible or God's Word, the Bible?

God will not contradict Himself. He did not give us two or more different ways to believe what He said in the Bible. If your beliefs contradict what the Bible says, then you have to question your beliefs.

The Bible is God-breathed, inspired by God, an inspiration of God, and given to man by God. Man did not come up with the Bible; God gave the Bible to man.

Do people believe a lot of things that are not true and not biblical about God? Yes, and they think their beliefs are correct; that is why I am stating these last few paragraphs in this chapter. All biblical doctrine should lineup with what the Bible says. Any doctrine that does not lineup with the Bible is not biblical and is not of/from God. Any and all biblical doctrine that someone teaches should be found in the Bible without being taken out of context. If you cannot find a belief in the Bible that is considered to be doctrinal, then it is not biblically correct and not a doctrine from God.

The Bible is complete. There is no need for new doctrine or new commands by some new prophet that is not in the Bible that would be supposedly from God. God will never change His laws, His commands, commandments, or His doctrine, nor will He give us new ones that are not in the Bible. God will never change the Bible. The Bible will never need to be updated to fit the modern times. It is the modern times that always need to be updated to the Bible.

The words may change because the meanings of the words have changed, but the meaning of the scripture has not changed. God is omniscient (all-knowing). God knew the times would change and He had the Bible written to always fit the present time, for all eternity. The Bible was, is, and always will be up to date with the present times, forever and forever. To not believe the Bible is to not believe God. The Bible was canonized so people would not believe and practice things that God does not want them to believe and practice. The reasons why other books are not in the Bible are because they do not meet all the canonizing requirements, and they are not inspired by God as His written Word. They have things in them that contradict the Bible.

Does God inspire men to write books today? Yes, and when it comes to doctrine, God inspires men to only write about what is written in the Bible. To teach what the Bible is saying, and to not come up with doctrine of his own or teach beliefs or doctrine of any kind that is not in the Bible.

Remember, many different English translations, worded differently, are *the* Bible, not Bibles. They all are the same Bible just worded differently, with the same meaning. They all have the same books, the same message, and the same doctrine, except for the Bible called The New World Translation of the Holy Scriptures and the Queen James Bible.

CHAPTER 3:

CONCEPTS AND BELIEFS OF THE BIBLE

We know people have different concepts and beliefs about the Bible, and we need to look at them to understand the differences. A couple of questions or comments are, "Mike, you've got your beliefs, and I've got mine." Or "Mike, you've got your ways, I've got mine." As you read the Scriptures that I will be showing you in this book, you will see it is not just my beliefs or ways but it is what God tells us to believe. There are religions or churches that teach wrong things about God. I ask, then, are your beliefs or ways coming directly from the Bible, or are they just hearsay?

Hearsay: meaning you never really looked in the Bible and checked to see for yourself if the verses that you were being shown really say what you are being taught. You believe what you are taught, but you do not know where it is in the Bible. You have no idea what the rest of the surrounding verses say, or if they back up the verses of what you are being shown. In other words, does the verse being shown have the same meaning as it has in the Bible? You never take time to read and study the Bible to see if what you believe is being taught correctly or not from the Bible. You do not know if your beliefs are phrases or verses being taken out of context or not. Without reading and studying the Bible for yourself, you accept whatever your church teaches.

Hearsay used to fit me perfectly. When I graduated from high school, I hated reading, studying, and writing. Then, a few years later, I found myself wanting to read the Bible. After reading and studying the Bible, I had to change my beliefs because I found out my beliefs were not correct according to the Bible. The beliefs I had were from phrases and verses that were taken out of context from the Bible. Some of my beliefs were not even in the Bible. Now, my beliefs line up with the scriptures in the Bible.

If you do not read the Bible, where do your beliefs come from? "Well, that is what my church believes," or "This is what my church teaches," or is it just hearsay from someone? I am not saying that all churches are wrong. I do not claim that one church has everything right and all the other churches are wrong. No one has a perfect church because we are human, and as humans, we are not perfect. "Well, then, why go to church?" Because by going to church, you can understand and learn a lot more about God, Jesus, and the Bible.

Please read on. Are your beliefs handed down from generation to generation? Are they in agreement with what the Bible really teaches or not? If not, then who is any man to say we should believe this way or that way if it is not in agreement with the Bible? If your beliefs are not in agreement with the Bible or are not in the Bible, then they are man-made beliefs and are not of or from God. God told us everything that He wants us to believe. God told us what to believe and what not to believe. God also tells us what He wants us to do and what He does not want us to do. It is *all* in the Bible, for us, and God has no contradictions in His Bible. If you find one, then you are misinterpreting one or some of the scriptures. God does not, and will not contradict Himself. Everything that God wants you to believe is in the Bible.

"Why do you say man-made beliefs are not in agreement with what the Bible really teaches?" Good question. Most man-made beliefs come from the Bible, but they are not in agreement with what the Bible is really teaching us. This is because a verse is being taken out of context to prove a belief that is not true. All our beliefs should be in agreement with the Bible because the Bible is the inspired Word of God.

"Mike, what if you are wrong and I am right?" Well, then, I will have lived a godly life according to the Bible and will have nothing to lose. But, I say to you, what if you are wrong and God's Word, the Bible, the Holy Scriptures is right? Then, you will have lost eternal life in heaven. The main question is this: is the verse or verses being used to prove your beliefs or mine beliefs being taken out of context or not? Please, at least hear God and me out.

"Mike, how can people come up with so many different religions or beliefs?" The main reason is Satan will do anything to get someone to believe the wrong way to keep them from going to heaven and to keep Christians from being united as one. Satan knows the Bible and even knows how to get believers to believe the wrong way. There are a lot of reasons why, but let's just look at some of the reasons.

Here are a few concepts and beliefs that some people have of the Bible that I have heard since 1972.

1. There are people who think it is too hard to live the way God wants us to live. They seem to accept only the beliefs that best suit the way they want to live,

and it seems like they think God is okay with that. Yes, it is not always easy to live a Christian life, but neither is life itself easy to live.

2. There are those who say man wrote the Bible, so you cannot believe everything that is in the Bible. Then, they use just the parts of the Bible that they want to believe and/or want you to believe. They will also take things out of context from the Bible to support their beliefs. (The Bible was given by the inspiration of God; does any person have the right to pick what to believe or what not to believe in the Bible? No!)

3. Unfortunately, I hate to admit it, but there are things in the Bible that can be interpreted more than one way. The problem with this is people tend to say this about doctrinal beliefs that cannot be interpreted more than one way. The result is doctrinal beliefs get twisted. That is why we have a lot of religions.

Look at how Satan can twist God's Word and deceive a believer.

Genesis 2:16–17, 3:1–5 (NIV)

[16] And the Lord God commanded the man, "You are free to eat from any tree in the garden;

[17] but you must not eat from the tree of the knowledge of good and evil, for when you eat from it you will certainly die."

[1]...Now the serpent was more crafty than any of the wild animals the Lord God had made. He said to the woman, "Did God really say, 'You must not eat from any tree in the garden'?"

[2] The woman said to the serpent, "We may eat fruit from the trees in the garden,

[3] but God did say, 'You must not eat fruit from the tree that is in the middle of the garden, and you must not touch it, or you will die.'"

[4] "You will not certainly die," the serpent said to the woman.

[5] "For God knows that when you eat from it your eyes will be opened, and you will be like God, knowing good and evil."

God said to Adam that he could eat of every tree in the garden except the tree of the knowledge of good and evil. Then Satan came to Eve and asked, "Did God say you cannot eat of every tree of the garden?" Notice what God said and then how Satan tried to confuse Eve by changing or twisting what God said in his question to Eve.

In the King James version, when Eve corrected Satan's question, she said, "We may eat of the fruit of the trees of the garden: But of the fruit of the tree which is in the middle of the garden, God has said, you shall not eat of it, neither shall you touch it, lest you die." Satan got Eve confused just enough to get her to add something that God did not say; she said, "Neither shall you touch it."

When God said you will die if you eat from the tree of knowledge, God meant a spiritual death, not a physical death. Satan got Eve to believe it was physical death.

Then, Satan lies to Eve by saying to her, "You will not die if you eat of the tree of knowledge." Satan then tempts Eve with a temptation that she could not resist, "You shall be as gods, knowing good and evil."

With the help of his temptation, Satan got Eve to believe what he told her instead of believing what God said. Being as a god, knowing good and evil, was enough for Eve to not believe God and disobey God's Word.

The beliefs that a lot of religions have in common are that they believe the same way about being born again and what the Bible teaches about God, Jesus, and the Holy Spirit.

"Mike, what does it mean to take a verse out of context?" When a verse is used by itself, it still has the same meaning that it has when it is with its surrounding verses in the Bible. If a verse does not have the same meaning when a person is using it by itself, then it is being taken out of context. In reality, all verses have their same meaning no matter which verse it is. There are verses that do have more than one meaning because they are talking about more than one thing at the same time. A person misusing it usually is trying to say that the verse is talking about a different subject than what it is actually talking about in the Bible. This is one of the reasons why you need to read and study the Bible. To make sure that the verse is not being taken out of context and that the verse is saying what its subject is about. This way, you know if you are being conned or not. It is very easy to get someone to believe something wrong about God when that someone does not read and study the Bible for themselves.

It seems like whenever I try to talk about a doctrine that can be taken only one way, I get told, "Mike, that is just your interpretation of the Bible." When someone says, "That is just your interpretation of the Bible," it is like saying you cannot know for sure if you are right in what you believe. Your interpretation does not mean you are right. This statement is said by believers and non-believers alike. It is easy to deny what one is teaching or saying when one does not read and examine the verses that they are given. Can one say the verses being given are not saying what they are teaching or talking about without reading and examining them? The answer is no because without reading and studying the verses for themselves, one cannot say if he/she is right or not. There is no need for interpretation when one is given a stated fact or stated facts in the Bible. There are verses in the Bible that do have multiple meanings were one can get more than one meaning out of the verse, so you will get a lot of things out of a verse. That is why people can get two different meanings out of a verse, and the meanings do not contradict each other. One example is Psalm 22; it was written hundreds of years before Jesus was born. Inspired by God, David writes what he is feeling because of the things that are happening, referring this to him. But the significance of this passage also refers to Christ Jesus when He was dying on the cross.

People can get their *own* interpretation of the Scriptures when they take a verse or verses out of context or if it is too hard to understand. I try very hard to make sure that I am not taking verses out of context. That is why I say, "Read the Bible, so you know this is what the Bible verses are saying." That is just your interpretation of the verses in the Bible. This does *not* apply to every single verse and doctrine that is in the Bible. "That is just your interpretation of the verses in the Bible." "It all depends on how you look at it." There are certain verses in the Bible that these statements are true. However, these two statements are not true when it comes to the basic doctrinal beliefs that I talk about in this book. The common man can understand the Bible's basic doctrine when reading other translations besides the King James Version. When it comes to basic doctrinal beliefs, there are many separate, different reasons why anyone says these two statements, but only a couple of these reasons may apply to any one person when saying them.

Here are some of the reasons:

1. To not have to listen to what you are saying.
2. Thinking there are different ways you can interpret beliefs without misinterpreting the Scriptures.
3. They have no idea of what the Bible really says and no understanding of what the Bible is completely saying about the doctrine that they are talking about.

I do not believe I can or have touched on all of these reasons, and none of them fit everyone. Remember, not all of these reasons apply to a person when they say that is just your interpretation. Plus, these statements do not apply to all the verses in the Bible. There are doctrinal stated facts of beliefs in the Bible that can only be taken one way.

A person will say one of these two statements when they know their beliefs are being proved wrong by what is in the

Bible. They see the truth in the Bible and know they cannot say, "That is not what it is saying." They do not want to admit their belief is wrong. Then they want you to believe God is not precise on anything of what He says about the doctrinal beliefs in the Bible. Here are a few other reasons why someone will say one of these two statements.

1. They most likely are not born again and go by hearsay and have their own opinion without reading the Bible, thinking what they have been taught to believe is right. They do not know where their beliefs come from, so they say the Bible can be taken in different ways.

2. They read the Bible and do not understand what they read, so they think there is more than one way to interpret the Bible. (There is more than one way to interpret the Bible when a person takes the verses out of context and does not consider everything that is being said about a subject that is in the Bible.)

3. They do not study or read the Bible and think they are right when they say it all depends on how you look at the scriptures and interpret them.

4. Unfortunately, there are people who come up with their own interpretation without ever reading or studying the whole Bible. Again, they think they are correct when they say, "That is just your interpretation of the Bible," because they do not know all of what is in the Bible. They do not understand

the Bible, nor do they fully comprehend what they read in the Bible. They know they cannot say you are wrong. Therefore, they say, "That is just your interpretation of the verses in the Bible," or "It all depends on how you look at it."

Again and again, I hear people say the last two statements in number four, thinking these statements are true about everything in the Bible. I feel I cannot stress enough when it comes to stated facts of the basic beliefs how false these two statements are about the doctrine of the Bible on what it teaches.

"Mike, what do you mean by basic beliefs or basic doctrine?" I mean things like salvation, being born again, baptism, graven images, sin, repenting, the three being one God, and being a new creature in Christ. It is all the beliefs I talk about in this book and others that I did not talk about. It is the beliefs that the average common person may or may not believe in.

Another statement that people will say when they are being shown something from the Bible that says their belief is wrong is, "Mike, you were brainwashed to believe what you believe about God and the Bible." You can actually say that about anything that people are taught to believe. Everyone's brain was washed one way or another, and their brain was taught and influenced to believe what they believe. If I am brainwashed, it is the best brainwashing I ever had. With all the bad things going on in the world today from what people are taught to believe and do, a lot of people need a good brainwashing from the Bible. Especially those who think it is okay to do bad things to others and think nothing should be done to them. It is a good thing to wash your brain with the Bible.

If two people look at a verse and one person sees one thing and the other person sees something else, that is because the verse is talking about more than just one subject. If two people look at a verse and one person believes one thing and the other person believes the opposite, then one person is misinterpreting the verse. The Bible has only one interpretation of itself, not many when it comes to stated facts of what the Bible is saying. No, it is not just my interpretation; it is what the Bible says.

When it comes to basic beliefs, the Bible cannot be taken more than one way unless the verses are taken out of context or one is misinterpreting the verses. "Mike, but there are verses that can be interpreted more than one way." Yes, but we have to remember not every single verse or belief can be interpreted in more than one way. If you do not accept the whole Bible but only parts of it, then you will have an inaccurate interpretation of what the Bible says. God is not a God of confusion. When you accept the whole Bible, you can see that God has only one interpretation of many beliefs in the Bible. All the doctrines of the Bible are in agreement with each other. All the books in the Bible are in agreement with each other. It is not how one looks at it, and it is not my own interpretation of the Bible, but you will see it is what the Bible says.

To say that it is just your own interpretation means the person has not really read and studied the entire Bible on the subject or belief. They say that it is just your own interpretation because the verses they are being shown are saying their beliefs are wrong. This statement is a copout of not having to hear, read, or see the truth because their beliefs are being disproved, knowing they cannot dispute what is being shown to them. It is like saying that the proof that one has of what the Bible is saying is not what the Bible is saying.

Here is a ridiculous example, but it makes my point. One of the ten commandments is you shall not kill. This is clear. You conclude: I believe it is saying that God does not want us to kill. Then you are told, "That is just your own interpretation." Really? The reason the person is saying, "That is just your own interpretation," is because they believe that it is all right to kill. They also say it because they are being shown by the Bible that their belief is wrong, and they know they cannot dispute it. They cannot prove their belief is right; therefore, they say, "That is just your own interpretation."

"That is just your own interpretation," or "It all depends on how you look at it." These statements are usually said by those who do not want to admit that their beliefs are being proved wrong according to the Bible or do not want to accept what you are saying. It is the pride of saying, "I am right, and you cannot know for sure what you are saying," or "You are wrong because my beliefs are right." They think, *Even though you just showed me that the Bible says my beliefs are wrong, you cannot be right.* Yes! It does hurt deeply to be shown that our beliefs are wrong, according to the Bible. We have to believe the Bible is correct because the Bible is the inspired written Word of God.

How can anyone say, "That is just your own interpretation," or "It all depends on how you look at it," if they are not looking at the verses and seeing exactly what they are saying? These statements can only be true about stated facts in the Bible when someone is not willing to examine the verses on how they are worded. It is when they do not know all of what the Bible says about the belief. It is when they do not want to believe exactly what they are being told. People will say these statements because they believe they cannot misinterpret what they read in the Bible.

To say these two statements are true about everything or every belief in the Bible is to say God left it up to man how to believe all the doctrinal beliefs of the Bible. It is to say God lets man choose which way to believe, if he should believe this way or that way. It is like saying God decided to let man pick what man wants to believe and how man wants to believe. It all depends on how you interpret the verses. It is saying the Bible is not clear on anything about what we should believe. What this really means is that one has not made a thorough enough search for all the scripture on a doctrine of the Bible. This means one has not thoroughly paid enough attention to the wording of the scripture on a doctrine of the Bible. We have to look at the what, why, and how everything is said in the Bible.

Think about it. It is like saying God inspired man to write the Bible so each and every man can come up with his own interpretation of the whole Bible to pick and choose whatever and however man wants to believe about what God said. This is how the average man talks about everything in the Bible today, not wanting to accept any stated facts in the Bible because it may say their beliefs are wrong. No more need for discussion on anything in the Bible because that is just your interpretation of it. This is not how God wants us to believe what He had man write in the Bible.

Here is an example of how this works. You point out verses that prove Jesus is God. Without saying you don't know how to interpret it right, they say, "Well, that is just your interpretation. That really does not mean Jesus is God because it all depends on how you interpret the verses in the Bible." It is like saying you cannot know for sure if you are interpreting it right. They might as well say you are wrong in your interpretation. Even though it is not your interpretation, it is exactly what the verses are saying that you are pointing out to them. They do not want to accept it because that is not what they believe. So, that is just your interpretation.

I believe God never intended for every belief in the Bible to be interpreted in many different ways. Yet man, without thoroughly searching for all the scriptures on a doctrine and examining completely how each scripture is worded, comes up with different interpretations of the Bible. Man tries to interpret the Bible instead of accepting its stated facts. Basing man's beliefs on opinions and theories of what man thinks it is saying rather than on what the words of the Bible are saying.

I am just one of many Christians relaying the message of God, clarifying what God says in His Bible and about some of the things that are being taught wrongly about God in the world today. The Bible is clear on what we are to believe. Do not be conned; read your Bible, which is the manual God gave you on how to live your life. Who gave and inspired man to write the Bible? God did; it's His Bible.

"Mike, can man-made beliefs come from the Bible?" Yes, when a verse or verses are being taken out of context, man-made beliefs are formed from the Bible. A lot of man-made beliefs develop because of misinterpretations of the Bible. When a person or persons take Scriptures out of context and say, "This is what we should believe," it will undoubtedly result in false doctrine. They would sooner have people believe what their opinion is than teach the truth of what the Scripture is saying. Then, because people do not read the Bible and study it, they believe the man-made beliefs, which are all wrong. It seems like a certain percentage of the people who are shown the correct way of what to believe, which is backed up by the Scriptures, will still choose not to believe the Scriptures. This is the same as not believing God.

There are people who say, "You cannot believe everything in the Bible because it was written by man." Then, the same people will choose to believe man-made beliefs that are not in the Bible, that are written by man. What is wrong with this thinking? They do not think it through. The contradiction here is the statement or phrase "written by man." Without thinking of it, they are saying you cannot believe all of the doctrinal beliefs in the Bible because it was written by man. Then, they want you to believe all of their so-called doctrinal beliefs that are not in the Bible that are written by man.

The Bible was not written by man alone. Man did not come up with the doctrinal beliefs in the Bible. Man was inspired by God and was told what to write because man was moved by the Holy Spirit (2 Timothy 3:16; 2 Peter 1:20–21.) A lot of the books in the Bible were written many years apart, yet all the books are in agreement with each other. Men cannot stay in agreement for even a short period of time. Look at all the disagreements in the world today. This alone is a sign that God moved man by the Holy Spirit to write the Bible.

Do you want to know if you are being taught correctly or not about the Bible? The answer is easy: If you have not, you need to read and study the Bible for yourself. Later on, toward the end of this book, I will give you a list of New Testament books to read and the order in which to read them. As you read them, God will help you understand the Bible.

People will choose to believe that their religion is correct and not the Bible. This is mainly because a person will not check and read the Bible to see if they are being taught correctly or not. When a person is taught something all their life and then finds out what the Bible really says, it is sometimes hard for that person to change their beliefs.

Yes, it does hurt when someone can show you from the Bible that your beliefs are wrong. That is when you have to decide if you are going to continue to believe your man-made beliefs or to believe God's Word. God's Word is correct and man-made beliefs are not correct. Who is man to say that God and His Word are wrong? This is why you need to read the Bible so you know if you are being taught correctly or not according to the Bible. The Bible is what God wants us to believe.

"Well, this is what so and so says," or "This is what my church teaches." Can you find in the Bible exactly where it says what you are being taught? Is the wording or phrase from the Bible saying exactly what you are taught? Can you look in the Bible at the surrounding verses of the wording or phrase and say, "Yes, the verses are saying the same thing"? If not, then you are being taught incorrectly. If you cannot say yes because you do not know, then who is wrong—you or God's Word? When you take the whole Bible or the whole verse or verses, you will see exactly what God is teaching in the Bible. "Mike, how do we know if you are right or not?" By opening up the Bible and looking up the surrounding verses of the verses I am showing you and studying them.

I say again the Bible is God-breathed, inspired by God, an inspiration of God, and given to man by God. Man did not come up with the Bible; God gave the Bible to man. You do not have to be a scholar to understand things in the Bible. If you are born again and read a Bible in the English we speak today, you will understand the Bible.

The KJV was not translated from the original languages that the Bible was written in but from Latin only, and the other Bibles were translated from the original languages: Hebrew, Arabic, and Greek. My point is how can it be that the KJV is the only accurate Bible when it is the only Bible not translated from the original languages? One would think that other English translations would be more accurate because they were translated from the original languages. Fortunately, even though the KJV was translated from a different language other than what the Bible was written in, the KJV is an accurate Bible. The proof is when the other Bibles were translated hundreds of years later, that the verses still have the same meanings. What we call the doctrinal beliefs of the Bible are still the same in each Bible. God did not let the meanings of the verses be changed, nor did He let the doctrinal beliefs change.

There are those today who are saying the Bible does not apply to all of the things that are happening in the world today because we are more liberal and our lifestyles are different compared to biblical days.

According to the Bible, God is all-knowing. He made sure that the Bible would apply to all generations from the beginning of time to the end of time. There are people who think that because our laws have been changed to suit the liberal lifestyles of today, the Bible should not condemn these liberal lifestyles anymore because of the people's rights by law to live the way they want to live. Even though the law of the land allows things that were once wrong to be okay, it does not mean that God will change the Bible to make them okay. What was sin to God at the beginning of time is and will be sin to God at the end of time. God will never change the Bible to suit the liberal lifestyles of sin just because society has said it is okay to live that way.

We may do things differently today, but we still do the same sinful things they did back in biblical days. Times have changed, but the Bible still and will always apply to us today, no matter how advanced or liberal we have become. God, in His infinite wisdom, has given us a severe warning regarding making any changes in the Bible.

Deuteronomy 4:2 (ESV)

²You shall not add to the word that I command you, nor take from it, that you may keep the commandments of the Lord your God that I command you.

Revelation 22:18–19 (ESV)

¹⁸ I warn everyone who hears the words of the prophecy of this book: if anyone adds to them, God will add to him the plagues described in this book,

¹⁹ and if anyone takes away from the words of the book of this prophecy, God will take away his share in the tree of life and in the holy city, which are described in this book.

God is telling us that no one should add or take away the meanings of the words of the Bible or take away any of its prophecies. "So we do not suffer dire consequences or lose our salvation." God does not want the meaning of His commands in the Bible to ever be changed. God will never tell us to change the Bible. Never! God has inspired and given the Bible to last till the end of time. We need to be careful what we say is or is not in the Bible or what we say the Bible teaches. According to these verses, one better be right. Every person, even if they are not a Bible scholar, who teaches from the Bible will be held accountable by God to teach correctly what is in the Bible, and that includes me.

Just one more thing about the Bible in 2 Timothy 3:16 (AMP),

> [16] Every Scripture is God-breathed (given by His inspiration) and profitable for instruction, for reproof and conviction of sin, for correction of error and discipline in obedience, [and] for training in righteousness (in holy living, in conformity to God's will in thought, purpose, and action.)

I like how the Amplified Bible brings out a fuller meaning of this verse and other verses in the Bible. All Scripture is profitable for doctrine, "for instruction, for reproof and conviction of sin, for correction of error and discipline in obedience, [and] for training in righteousness (in holy living, in conformity to God's will in thought, purpose, and action)." This means everything we need to know is in the Scriptures: doctrine, instruction, reproof and conviction of sin, correction of error and discipline in obedience, training in righteousness, in holy living, and in conformity to God's will in thought, purpose, and action. It is all in the Bible. My point is that all biblical doctrine should always be in the Bible and from the Bible. We are to believe the doctrine of the Bible, not man-made doctrine from books that are not in the Bible or man-made doctrine that is taken out of context from the Bible.

The New Testament was canonized by the councils of the third century, and the Bible was complete by the fifth century, so we would not accept, believe, and practice things that are not written in the Bible. It is said that it was not until or around the sixteenth century that a few books of the Old Testament were taken out of the Bible because it was found that they had some contradictions in them. How true that is, I do not know. One's concepts and beliefs should come from and line up with the Bible. One's beliefs should not be their opinion or their own interpretation, but their beliefs should be based on what is written in the Bible. Beliefs that do not line up with the Bible are false.

It is said that you cannot believe everything in the Bible because you know how a sentence can change from one person to the next, and by the tenth or twentieth person, the sentence will have changed. The same is said about the manuscripts of the Bible. I have to ask, if this is supposed to be true about the Bible, then why is it not true about historical history that was written over and over again by man from over a thousand years ago? The difference between the two is that historical history was only written by man. The Bible was written by man who was inspired by God our creator, where God Himself told man what to write. God, who is all-knowing and all-powerful, is not going to let His Bible be changed over the years.

If historical history that was written by man did not change, then the Bible did not change either. History books have been written over and over again. You cannot believe all of our historical history because you know how a sentence can change from one person to the next, and by the tenth or twentieth person, the sentence will have changed. Yet, those who said this about the Bible believe everything of historical history that was written by man. If you can believe all of our historical history that was written by man long ago, then you can believe all of the Bible that was written by man long ago.

It is really something how people who have never read and studied the whole Bible or any part of it believe themself to be and/or talk like they are more of an authority on the Bible than people who actually read and study the Bible. How can anyone know what they are talking about and think they are an authority on the Bible if they have never read it? The answer is that they do not know. I rest my case.

CHAPTER 4:

THE LOVE OF GOD AND JESUS FOR YOU

It is a part of being born again to know and understand God's love for you and what Jesus Christ willingly went through for you. Let's talk about God's love for you. No matter who you are or what you are, God loves you.

> John 3:16–17 (NIV)
>
> [16] For God so loved the world [so much] that he gave his one and only Son, that whoever believes in him shall not perish but have eternal life.
>
> [17] For God did not send his Son into the world to condemn [judge] the world, but to save the world through him.

Looking at these two verses, we are going to personalize them because God loves everybody. In verse 16, it says, "God so loved the world." When Jesus said "the world," He was talking about every single person on this planet, calling everybody the world, past, present, and future. "For God so loved the world," for God so loved you. You can put your name there. It is because He loves you that He gave His Son just for you, that you might be saved. That is a lot of love. How many people do you know that would give their son's life for you to be saved because they love you? I believe there is no one else who would give up their son's life for you to be saved.

"Mike, why do you say so I might be saved?" That is a good question. God does not decide who gets saved. The decision is ours, not God's. We make the decision by what we choose to do here on Earth regarding whether or not we will go to heaven. You will understand this after reading what it means to be born again.

Think about it. God willingly let His own Son be sacrificed for you so you can have eternal life and live in heaven forever. This is how God demonstrated His love towards us.

Romans 5:8 (NIV)

> [8] But God demonstrates his own love for us in this:
> While we were still sinners, Christ died for us.

Jesus died for you. God demonstrated His own love to us, to save us, by letting Jesus die on the cross for us. God demonstrated His own love to save you while you were still sinning against Him. Jesus did it all for you. God the Father loves you! God the Son (Jesus) loves you! God and Jesus want you to have eternal life. They want you to go to heaven and not to hell.

Before Jesus Christ was arrested, He knew what was going to happen to Him. Jesus foretold His death in Matthew 20:17-19 (NIV),

> [17] Now Jesus was going up to Jerusalem. On the way, he took the Twelve aside [privately] and said to them,

> ¹⁸ "We are going up to Jerusalem, and the Son of Man will be delivered over to the chief priests and the teachers of the [religious] law. They will condemn [sentence] him to death
>
> ¹⁹ and will hand him over to the Gentiles [Romans] to be mocked and flogged [with a whip] and crucified. On the third day he will be raised to life [from the dead]!"

Jesus knew He was going to be beaten, whipped, then beaten again, and crucified. He knew the pain and agony that He was going to have to go through for you. Jesus also knew He had to go through this because He had to make the way for us to go to heaven. There was and is no other way. Anyone who is not Jewish is a Gentile.

John 1:1 (AMP)

> ¹ In the beginning [before all time] was the Word (Christ), and the Word was with God, and the Word was God Himself.

This is how it is worded in Greek, "In the beginning was the Word, and the Word was with God, and God was the Word." Truly this verse is saying that Jesus is God. Jesus is God the Son. Jesus, God the Son being in human form, knew that He was going to feel all of the agonizing pain just like anyone else would. Just like any other human, He did not want to go through all that pain, so He prayed this prayer:

> Mark 14:36 (AMP)
>
> ³⁶ And He was saying, Abba, [which means] Father, everything is possible for You. Take away this cup from Me; yet not what I will, but what You [will].

Jesus knew that every sin that was ever committed or would be committed would be on Him. He knew our fate was resting on Him to go through with this cup of suffering. If you read Isaiah chapter 53, Jesus knew this was about Him and what He would have to bear when He died on the cross for us. He had our sins, our transgressions, our iniquities, and the chastisement for our peace was upon Him when He died. Jesus was facing a painful, bitter death, but He knew He had to face it for us. Keep this in mind as you read of His love for you. He did it for you because He loves you. I will touch later on another reason why He prayed that prayer.

Jesus knew that besides the pain He was going to experience, He was going to let Himself be shamed and humiliated before everyone. Jesus did not really want to physically experience all the agonizing pain that He knew He was going to have to go through, either. But if this is the only way that you could be saved, and because of His love for you, He was willing and did go through it for you. In Jesus' prayer, He said, "Father, all things are possible for You. Please take this cup from Me."

What Jesus was saying is, "God, You can do anything. Don't let Me die on the cross. Don't have Me go through all that agonizing pain, but—" but Jesus said, "But if it is Your will, I will do it." It was God's will for Jesus to go through all the agonizing pain for you (us) and to die on the cross for you (us); all of this is the cup that Jesus was talking about. Jesus willingly took the physical agonizing pain for you (us) because He loves you (us).

The next thing I want to point out to you is Jesus was physically a strong man. He was not a thin, skinny man. He had a body of strong physical strength. Jesus was a carpenter before He started His ministry. He was a well-known carpenter because He was recognized as such when He began to teach on the Sabbath in the synagogue. If you open your Bible, in reading Mark 6:1-2, Jesus began to teach in the synagogue. Verse 3 says this:

Mark 6:3 (ESV)

³ "Is not this the carpenter, the son of Mary and brother of James and Joses and Judas and Simon? And are not his sisters here with us?" And they took offense at him.

Luke 3:23 (ESV)

²³ Jesus, when he began his ministry, was about thirty years of age, being the son (as was supposed) of Joseph, the son of Heli.

As we can see, the people knew who Jesus was. They knew who His parents were, and they knew who His brothers and sisters were, and they knew Jesus as just a carpenter. Jesus must have done a lot of carpentry work because they all knew He was just a carpenter. They pointed out His parents and siblings because of how deeply offended they were by this carpenter. They did this to discredit Jesus.

The Passover is celebrated only once a year. It is only through John's mentioning of the Passovers that we can estimate the age of Jesus when He died on the cross. John mentions three Passovers occurring once Jesus' ministry started. And a fourth one occurred during His death on the cross. After careful reading and studying, the Sabbath following the calibration of the Passover is always a special Sabbath because of the Passover. The Jews do not want people on the cross of that particular Sabbath.

John 2:23 (ESV)

²³ Now when he was in Jerusalem at the Passover Feast, many believed in his name when they saw the signs that he was doing.

John 6:4 (ESV)

⁴ Now the Passover, the feast of the Jews, was at hand.

John 11:55–57 (ESV)

⁵⁵ Now the Passover of the Jews was at hand, and many went up from the country to Jerusalem before the Passover to purify themselves.

⁵⁶ They were looking for Jesus and saying to one another as they stood in the temple, "What do you think? That he will not come to the feast at all?"

⁵⁷ Now the chief priests and the Pharisees had given orders that if anyone knew where he was, he should let them know, so that they might arrest him.

John 19:31 (ESV)

> ³¹ Since it was the day of Preparation, and so that the bodies would not remain on the cross on the Sabbath (for that Sabbath was a high day), the Jews asked Pilate that their legs might be broken and that they might be taken away.

Notice in the Gospel of John that there were three Jewish Passovers recorded after Jesus turned thirty and started His ministry. A fourth Passover was recorded right when He died. This proves that Jesus was no older than thirty-four when He was arrested and died on the cross. Looking back at Mark 6:3 and at the age of Jesus, He was a strong young man. He was not Mr. America or Hercules, but He was a strong young man. "Mike, how can you say that Jesus was a physically strong man from these verses?" I'm glad you asked that question. Back in Jesus' day, carpenters did not have any electrical tools or a local lumber yard like Menards or Home Depot to go to.

The power that His tools had came from His arms and hands. He may have carried 6x6 beams on His shoulders because there were no forklifts or trucks. Jesus must have done a lot of carpentry work. Why else would the people say, "Is this not the carpenter?" They also knew His whole family. Just like Menards and Home Depot are well known, Jesus was well known as Jesus the carpenter, Son of Joseph and Mary. Jesus had to be a strong person to survive what He went through before He was nailed to the cross. Now that I said all of that, I can tell you of the great love that Jesus has for the world, for us, for you!

In reading Matthew 26, before we get to verse 47, we read that Jesus was talking to His disciples who were tired because of how late at night it was.

Matthew 26:47–54 (NIV)

[47] While he was still speaking, Judas, one of the Twelve, arrived. With him was a large crowd armed with swords and clubs, sent from the chief priests and elders of the people.

[48] Now the betrayer had arranged a signal with them: "The one I kiss is the man; arrest him."

[49] Going at once to Jesus, Judas said, "Greetings, Rabbi!" and kissed him.

[50] Jesus replied, "Do what you came for, friend." Then the men stepped forward, seized Jesus and arrested him.

[51] With that, one of Jesus' companions reached for his sword, drew it out and struck the servant of the high priest, cutting off his ear.

[52] "Put your sword back in its place," Jesus said to him, "for all who draw the sword will die by the sword.

[53] Do you think I cannot call on my Father, and he will at once put at my disposal more than twelve legions of angels?

[54] But how then would the Scriptures be fulfilled that say it must happen in this way?"

When Jesus was arrested, He knew at any given time that He could call out to God the Father, and over twelve legions of angels would come and rescue Him. Jesus also knew that if He did cry out, we would not have a way to go to heaven. What great love for us! What great love for you! Jesus did it for us. Jesus did it for you. Jesus loves you. God loves you. God watched Jesus go through it all knowing He could have saved Jesus from it with over twelve legions of angels that were just waiting to rescue Jesus from all the pain. This is the great, wonderful, incredible, magnificent, awesome, and fantastic love that God and Jesus have for you. It is what you will be reading about in this chapter. This is just the tip of the iceberg of God's and Jesus' love for you. If there were any other way for us to go to heaven, then Jesus would not have had to die on the cross; His death would have been in vain. *But* Jesus had to pay the price for our salvation. Jesus Himself was that price.

As we read in Matthew 26:51, one of Jesus' companions reached for his sword, drew it out, and cut off the ear of one of the high priest's servants. We read that Jesus healed that servant. What love Jesus had to heal the one who was arresting Him.

Luke 22:51 (ESV)

[51] But Jesus said, "No more of this!" And he touched his ear and healed him.

The point is Jesus showed His love even to the ones who arrested Him.

Now that Jesus was arrested, let's go to Matthew 26:59–68 (NIV),

> [59] The chief priests and the whole Sanhedrin were looking for false evidence against Jesus so that they could put him to death.
>
> [60] But they did not find any, though many false witnesses came forward. Finally two came forward
>
> [61] and declared, "This fellow said, 'I am able to destroy the temple of God and rebuild it in three days.'"
>
> [62] Then the high priest stood up and said to Jesus, "Are you not going to answer? What is this testimony that these men are bringing against you?"
>
> [63] But Jesus remained silent. The high priest said to him, "I charge you under oath by the living God: tell us if you are the Messiah, the Son of God."
>
> [64] "You have said so," Jesus replied, "But I say to all of you: From now on you will see the Son of Man sitting at the right hand of the Mighty One and coming on the clouds of heaven."
>
> [65] Then the high priest tore his clothes and said, "He has spoken blasphemy! Why do we need any more witnesses? Look, now you have heard the blasphemy.
>
> [66] What do you think?" "He is worthy of death," they answered.
>
> [67] Then they spit in his face and struck him with their fists. Others slapped him
>
> [68] and said, "Prophesy to us, Messiah. Who hit you?"

Think about it: the chief priests, the high priest, the elders, and all the council (the whole Sanhedrin) did not believe that Jesus was the Christ. They knew and understood that Jesus said that He is the Son of God making Himself equal with God. Remember, these are scholars, teachers, and upholders of the Word of God, the Scriptures, or the Old Testament. This shows that even the men of God are not perfect. They, too, can make mistakes just like anyone else. In this case, the chief priests, the elders, and all the council were breaking one of the ten commandments. "Thou shalt not bear false witness against thy neighbor." Plus the fact they did not believe Jesus. They were trying to find false witnesses against Jesus. And these were scholars of the Word of God. They wanted Jesus dead even before they decided to arrest Him. The Jews sought to kill Jesus because He said He was the Son of God, making Himself equal with God. We see that in the verses below,

John 5:17–18 (NIV)

[17] Jesus said to them, "My Father is always at his work to this very day, and I too am working."

[18] For this reason they tried all the more to kill him; not only was he breaking the Sabbath, but he was even calling God his own Father, making himself equal with God.

The Jews accused Jesus of speaking blasphemy. The definition of blasphemy:

1. It is an act of insulting or showing contempt or lack of reverence for God.

2. The act of claiming the attributes of deity with God (being equal with God)

In Jesus' case, He was being accused of claiming the attributes of deity, that He was God. They knew this was exactly what Jesus meant, which was why the Jews wanted to kill Him. So in Matthew 26:65-68, when the high priest tore his clothes, it was in a sense of shame for God because Jesus was making Himself equal to God. We read in Luke 22:64 that they blindfolded Jesus and demanded Him to prophesy to them who hit Him. When they started to hit Jesus, they asked Him, "Who hit You?" If Jesus was equal with God, then He should know who was hitting Him.

Isaiah 50:6 (AMP)

⁶ I gave My back to the smiters and My cheeks to those who plucked off the hair; I hid not My face from shame and spitting.

This verse is about Jesus. It is about just one of the things that happened to Him after He was arrested. Smiters are people who practice killing with the punch of their fists. Smite means to try to kill by striking heavily with a heavy blow of the fist or hand. Jesus was hit many times by smiters. This verse also said Jesus would have His beard pulled off, and His face would be spit on. When they did all of this to Jesus, He did not turn His face away from them.

As we read earlier in Matthew 26:67, they were beating the tar out of Jesus. They spit in His face, and they hit Him. The King James says they buffeted and smote him. What do buffet and smote mean? "Buffet" is to pound repeatedly with the striking of the palm of the hand or fist. It also means fighting violently against your opponent. "Smote" is the past tense of smite, as we read earlier, smite means to try to kill by striking heavily with a heavy blow of the fist or hand.

Now, the point that I want to make is that Jesus is really taking a beating here in verse 67 of Matthew chapter 26. He is really getting the tar beaten out of Him. Jesus was being violently punched again and again. They were pounding on Him repeatedly with the intent to kill, striking Him over and over, again and again. Hitting Him as hard as they could, one violent punch after another, they took their rage out on Him. Jesus willingly allowed this to happen to Himself because of His love for you. Jesus' love for you kept Him from calling over twelve legions of angels to rescue Him. Jesus loves you so much that He allowed Himself to be violently beaten with the palms of their hands and fists with repeated blows. That is a lot of love! Jesus loves you! Jesus silently said, "I love you!"

Jesus has just taken a violent beating, and that was not the end of it. Let's read on Matthew 27:1–2 (NIV),

> [1] Early in the morning, all the chief priests and the elders of the people made their plans how to have Jesus executed.
>
> [2] So they bound him, led him away and handed him over to Pilate the governor.

After beating the tar out of Jesus, they took Jesus to Pilate in hopes that Pilate would sentence Jesus to death. They eventually did not give Pilate a choice.

Matthew 27:11–26 (ESV)

¹¹ Now Jesus stood before the governor, and the governor asked him, "Are you the King of the Jews?" Jesus said, "You have said so."

¹² But when he was accused by the chief priests and elders, he gave no answer.

¹³ Then Pilate said to him, "Do you not hear how many things they testify against you?"

¹⁴ But he gave him no answer, not even to a single charge, so that the governor was greatly amazed.

¹⁵ Now at the feast the governor was accustomed to release for the crowd any one prisoner whom they wanted.

¹⁶ And they had then a notorious prisoner called Barabbas.

¹⁷ So when they had gathered, Pilate said to them, "Whom do you want me to release for you: Barabbas, or Jesus who is called Christ?"

¹⁸ For he knew that it was out of envy that they had delivered him up.

¹⁹ Besides, while he was sitting on the judgment seat, his wife sent word to him, "Have nothing to do with that righteous man, for I have suffered much because of him today in a dream."

²⁰ Now the chief priests and the elders persuaded the crowd to ask for Barabbas and destroy Jesus.

²¹ The governor again said to them, "Which of the two do you want me to release for you?" And they said, "Barabbas."

²² Pilate said to them, "Then what shall I do with Jesus who is called Christ?" They all said, "Let him be crucified!"

²³ And he said, "Why? What evil has he done?" But they shouted all the more, "Let him be crucified!"

²⁴ So when Pilate saw that he was gaining nothing, but rather that a riot was beginning, he took water and washed his hands before the crowd, saying, "I am innocent of this man's blood; see to it yourselves."

²⁵ And all the people answered, "His blood be on us and on our children!"

²⁶ Then he released for them Barabbas, and having scourged Jesus, delivered him to be crucified.

Pilate believed that Jesus was innocent, and so did his wife because of her tormenting dream. Pilate did not believe any of the charges that Jesus was being accused of, and he knew Jesus did not break any Roman laws. Pilate did what he could to get Jesus released. Pilate picked the worst criminal he had, which was Barabbas. Who would want a notorious criminal released? Pilate thought for sure the people would pick Jesus over Barabbas. But as we read, the chief priests and the elders of the people persuaded the crowd to have Barabbas released and to have Jesus crucified. Pilate did not have a choice. He had to give the people what they wanted, because that is how it was at that time. But Pilate did not sentence Jesus; our sins did. There had to be a price paid for our sins, and Jesus was that price. Pilate gave the people what they asked for and wanted. He released Barabbas and had Jesus whipped and put to death.

Deuteronomy 25:1–3 (NIV)

¹ When people have a dispute, they are to take it to court and the judges will decide the case, acquitting the innocent and condemning the guilty.

² If the guilty person deserves to be beaten, the judge shall make them lie down and have them flogged in his presence with the number of lashes the crime deserves,

³ but the judge must not impose more than forty lashes. If the guilty party is flogged more than that, your fellow Israelite will be degraded in your eyes.

Note: The apostle Paul writes in 2 Corinthians 11:24 (NIV),

²⁴ Five times I received from the Jews the forty lashes minus one.

Think about it. The apostle Paul was whipped thirty-nine lashes five different times. What a commitment. Thank God that all those whippings did not keep Paul from writing the books of his that we have in our Bible today. Boy, you think you got it rough. Read 2 Corinthians chapter 11 and see all of what Paul went through.

Now, the Romans did not practice the law of the Jews. But in studying Roman history in Jesus' time period, the Romans did whip the prisoners while questioning and interrogating them. That is how the Romans would get the prisoners to say what they wanted to hear. After the thirty-ninth time, they would stop whipping the prisoner so he or she would stay alive long enough to be crucified. There was always the possibility of the prisoners bleeding to death before they would be done whipping them. The person doing the whipping had to be careful not to cut a main artery so that the person being whipped would not bleed to death. This is because of the type of whip that was being used. Jesus was being whipped with a lead-ripped whip.

Because Jesus kept silent when He was being questioned, most scholars believe that Jesus was whipped the whole thirty-nine times.

As Jesus was being whipped, He knew that the angels were waiting for His command to rescue Him. Jesus was already in a lot of pain (as He took the first stroke of the whip) from the beating He took before He was brought to Pilate.

Note: No one knows what Jesus was thinking after He was arrested. No one knows what was going through His mind while He was being beaten, whipped, and nailed to the cross. The following statements of what Jesus thought will not be found in the Scriptures. It is, instead, this author's opinion, after careful consideration of our Savior's character and what He accomplished by willingly going to the cross, that this is what Jesus may have thought while being whipped. The numbers represent each time He was whipped. Jesus willingly went through this for you because He loves you.

Each time Jesus was whipped, He may have thought or silently said, "I must continue to let them whip Me so that the Scriptures will be fulfilled."

One and...two! He felt the pain on top of the pain that He already had. Jesus thought and silently said, "I love *you!*" Three, four, and...five! The whip started to cut His skin open. Jesus silently said, "I love *you!*" Six, seven, and...eight! His blood started to squirt out. Jesus silently said, "I love *you!*" Nine and... ten! Jesus could feel the sharp pain from the whip as it sliced and cut His flesh. Jesus silently said, "I love *you!*"

Eleven, twelve, and...thirteen! The whip started to pull and tear the outer layer of skin away. Jesus silently said, "I love *you!*" Fourteen and...fifteen! Jesus thought, *I must not call the angels*, and silently said, "I love *you!*" Sixteen, seventeen, and... eighteen! Pilate may have asked each time, "Are You king of the Jews?" Jesus silently said, "I love *you!*"

Nineteen, twenty, and...twenty-one! Jesus' blood is spraying all over as the whip hits Him. Jesus silently said, "I love *you!*" Twenty-two, twenty-three, and...twenty-four! More flesh is being torn away. Jesus silently said, "I love *you!*" Twenty-five and...twenty-six! The pain is becoming so unbearable, and Jesus silently said, "I love *you!*" Twenty-seven, twenty-eight, and... twenty-nine! Jesus thought, *I have to let them continue to whip Me, for it is by My stripes that they are healed.* And Jesus silently said, "I love *you!*"

Thirty, thirty-one, and....thirty-two! More flesh was being torn away. Jesus silently said, "I love *you!*" Thirty-three and... thirty-four! By now, you could see Jesus' muscles beneath His flesh. Jesus silently said, "I love *you!*" Thirty-five and...thirty-six! The tissue of His muscles was being torn off, and as

Jesus could feel the agonizing pain, He silently said, "I love *you!*" Thirty-seven and…thirty-eight! God, holding back, would not and did not give the angels the command to rescue Jesus. As God watched Him, His only Son, being whipped, God and Jesus silently said, "I love *you!*"

As Jesus was being whipped, feeling all the horrifying pain, He was thinking of you. Jesus knew He had to go through this for you. Jesus knew this was the only way He could save you, and silently said, *"I love you!"* As Jesus took the last hit, thirty-nine, Jesus was thinking of *you* and silently said, *"I love you!"*

Each and every time Jesus was hit with the whip (all thirty-nine times), Jesus most likely thought of you and silently and physically said, "*I love you!*" Jesus' skin, His flesh and blood, the tissue of His muscles lying there on the ground. The agony, the unbearable pain, which all could have been avoided by just calling the angels to rescue Him, but God and Jesus silently said, "*I love you!*" Jesus knew He had to be whipped for *you*, for "by His stripes you were [and are] healed." Jesus silently said, "*I love you!*"

Isaiah 53:5 (ESV)

⁵ But he was pierced for our transgressions; he was crushed for our iniquities; upon him was the chastisement that brought us peace, and with his wounds we are healed.

Jesus silently said, "*I love you!*" I believe this verse speaks loudly for itself of what Jesus did for us. Jesus silently said, "*I love you!*" Thank You, Jesus.

Going back to Matthew 27:26, Pilate released Barabbas and ordered Jesus to be whipped and then crucified. After Jesus was whipped, the soldiers took Him away to be crucified. But they did not crucify Him right away.

Let's read Matthew 27:27–30 (NIV),

> [27] Then the governor's soldiers took Jesus into the Praetorium and gathered the whole company of soldiers around him.
>
> [28] They stripped him and put a scarlet robe on him,
>
> [29] and then twisted together a crown of thorns and set it on his head. They put a staff in his right hand. Then they knelt in front of him and mocked him, "Hail, king of the Jews!" they said.
>
> [30] They spit on him, and took the staff and struck him on the head again and again.

After Jesus was brutally and violently whipped, He was taken away by some of Pilate's Roman soldiers. Now, in a soldier's mind, if a prisoner is to be executed, the person is an enemy of the state or country. In today's world or in some countries, prisoners are to be treated with respect. In Jesus' days, prisoners were not treated with respect. No matter what country a soldier was serving in, the soldier was trained and taught to hate their enemy. It helps bring out the killing instinct in them for when they go to war. Unfortunately, at times, it brings out the worst. In Jesus' case, the soldiers may have said, "This man (enemy) thinks He is the king of the Jews. Let's have some fun with Him before we crucify Him." "Yeah, go get the rest of the men."

So, they called or gathered a "whole band of soldiers" (KJV) or a "whole company of soldiers" (NIV). In two other Bibles, "the whole battalion" (AMP) or "an entire regiment" (NLT). Anyway, it was a lot of soldiers.

They made a crown of thorns and put it on Jesus' head. They most likely pushed the crown down on His head so it would pierce His skin. They then took His clothes off and put a robe on Him. Then they put a staff in His right hand so Jesus would look the part of someone important. Now, Jesus is ready to be mocked. I am sure that they did not get a whole army of soldiers together just for them to watch one or two soldiers take the staff and hit Jesus. I believe that most of those soldiers got to take their turn in kneeling before Jesus and hailing Him as king of the Jews. Then took the staff from His right hand, smote Him on the head, and put the staff back in His right hand for the next soldier to be able to do the same. It is more fun to do the fun than it is to just watch.

They also spit on Him. Can you imagine a lot of soldiers spitting on your face one after another? This is what happened to Jesus. According to Isaiah 50:6, as we read earlier, Jesus also had His beard pulled off His face. Once again, but now by the soldiers, Jesus was violently beaten. This is after being whipped with a lead-ripped whip where His flesh and muscles were torn apart. These are Roman soldiers who are beating Jesus. They are trained very well in hand-to-hand combat and wield a sword for hours in a battle. These Roman soldiers are hitting Jesus on the head with a staff as hard as they can hit. For a second time, Jesus is getting the tar beaten out of Him, and worse than the first time. This went on and on until they decided that they had enough fun with Him. Jesus silently said, *"I love you!"*

Jesus' actions spoke louder than words. As we know, Jesus did not call the angels to rescue Him because He loves you. As He took the beating, the torture, the humiliation, and physically agonizing unbearable pain, He silently said, *"I love you!"*

Besides being strong, Jesus had to have had an anointing from God to be able to survive the beatings He took. He went through this for you and silently said, *"I love you!"* Jesus Christ's love for you is more *awesome* than anything in the world. "What happened next?"

> Matthew 27:31–34 (ESV),
>
> [31] And when they had mocked him, they stripped him of the robe and put his own clothes on him and led him away to crucify him.
>
> [32] As they went out, they found a man of Cyrene, Simon by name. They compelled this man to carry his cross.
>
> [33] And when they came to a placed called Golgotha (which means Place of a Skull),
>
> [34] they offered him wine to drink, mixed with gall, but when he tasted it, he would not drink it.

Now that the soldiers were done having fun beating Jesus, they took the robe off Him. While the soldiers were beating Jesus, His blood had probably started to dry to the muscles and the skin (of what was left) and had attached the muscles and skin to the robe, forming a scab. When you put on any type of clothing on an open wound, the clothes tend to stick to the open wound. They were not gentle when they took the robe off Jesus, and it most likely tore open the wounds on His body, and they started to bleed all over again. Then, they put His clothes back on Him and led Him away to be crucified. When a person was being led to the place where they were going to be crucified, they had to carry their own cross. Jesus was so tired, His strength so physically drained from the two brutal beatings He took, from the whipping, and the loss of blood that He had no strength left to carry the cross. This is why they forced the man called Simon to carry His cross.

> Matthew 27:35–37 (ESV)
>
> [35] And when they had crucified him, they divided his garments among them by casting lots.
>
> [36] Then they sat down and kept watch over him there.
>
> [37] And over his head they put the charge against him, which read, "This is Jesus, the King of the Jews."

Before they nailed Jesus to the cross, they took His clothes off Him. He was totally naked when He was hanging on the cross. After the soldiers took Jesus' clothes off, they lay Him down on the cross. They most likely did not have a smooth surface on the cross, but a rough, rugged cross that His open-wounded back was lying on. The soldiers took one hand and nailed it to the cross. Jesus felt the pain from the spike as it went through His hand and into the wood of the cross. Jesus silently said, "I love you!" Each time they hit the spike, He felt it going through His hand until it was deep enough into the cross. Jesus silently said,

"I love you!" Then, they took His other hand and nailed it to the cross. Again, He felt the spike pierce the flesh of His hand and the excruciating pain as He felt the spike go through His hand until the spike was deep enough into the cross. Jesus silently said, "I love you!"

Then, they took His feet and put them one on top of the other and started to drive a big, long spike into His feet. First, piercing the skin of the top foot and going through the muscle of His foot, now coming out the bottom of His foot and into His other foot. Jesus silently said, "I love you!" Again, piercing His skin, then His muscle, and coming out the bottom of His second foot and into the wood of the cross. Feeling the excruciating pain as the spike went through His feet, crushing them together until the spike was deep enough into the wood of the cross. Jesus silently said, "I love you!" Again, Jesus' actions spoke louder than words. Jesus did not call for the angels, and He silently said, "I love you!"

Note: There are those who will say they put the spikes through His wrist instead of His hands because of the weight of the body. Why would the gospel say the hands instead of the wrist if that were so? Think about it: would the wrist be that much stronger to hold the weight of the body than the hands? I don't think so.

The soldiers probably tied Jesus' arms to the cross because the tissues of the hand is not strong enough to hold the weight of the body on a cross. The hand would have ripped off of the spikes. Now that Jesus was nailed to the cross, they stood it up by putting the cross in a hole in the ground, and it most likely jolted Jesus' body, creating more pain.

As Jesus was hanging on the cross, His back was still torn open, and He had wide-open cuts of the flesh up against the rough wooden cross, His face beyond recognition from all of the hits He sustained from being smitten with their hands, fists, and the staff. His face was bleeding—red from the blood where His beard once was. His whole body was in pain beyond imagination, agonizing and in excruciating pain. Jesus silently said, "I love you!" He did not call for the angels to come and rescue Him. Jesus thought of you and just silently said, "I love you!"

Matthew 27:45–46 (ESV)

⁴⁵ Now from the sixth hour there was darkness over all the land until the ninth hour.

⁴⁶ And about the ninth hour Jesus cried out with a loud voice, saying, "Eli, Eli, lema sabachtani?" that is, "My God, my God, why have you forsaken me?"

Isaiah 53:5 (ESV)

"⁵ But he was pierced for our transgressions; he was crushed for our iniquities; upon him was the chastisement that brought us peace, and with his wounds we are healed."

Second Corinthians 5:21 (ESV)

"²¹ For our sake he made him to be sin who knew no sin, so that in him we might become the righteousness of God."

When Jesus cried out to God—"My God, My God, why have You forsaken or abandoned me?"—Jesus had all of the sins of the world on Him. From day one, everyone who lived and died before Him, who lived and died during His time, and who would live and die after Him. The whole world, from the beginning of time until the world's end of time, all of our sins, my sins, your sins, all our sins were on Him. Because God cannot stand sin, He forsook or abandoned Jesus when He was on the cross. It was our sins that made God forsake Jesus that day. But at the same time, God the Father and God the Son (Jesus) silently said, "I love you!" What an awesome love for you. God and Jesus endured this for you.

John 19:28–37 (ESV)

[28] After this, Jesus, knowing that all was now finished, said (to fulfill the Scripture), "I thirst."

[29] A jar full of sour wine stood there, so they put a sponge full of the sour wine on a hyssop branch and held it to his mouth.

[30] When Jesus had received the sour wine, he said, "It is finished," and he bowed his head and gave up his spirit.

[31] Since it was the day of Preparation, and so that the bodies would not remain on the cross on the Sabbath (for that Sabbath was a high day), the Jews asked Pilate that their legs might be broken and that they might be taken away.

[32] So the soldiers came and broke the legs of the first, and of the other who had been crucified with him.

³³ But when they came to Jesus and saw that he was already dead, they did not break his legs.

³⁴ But one of the soldiers pierced his side with a spear, and at once there came out blood and water.

³⁵ He who saw it has borne witness—his testimony is true, and he knows that he is telling the truth—that you also may believe.

³⁶ For these things took place that the Scripture might be fulfilled: "Not one of his bones will be broken."

³⁷ And again another Scripture says, "They will look on him whom they have pierced."

Jesus knew He won the battle. He knew the Scriptures were fulfilled, so He said, "It is finished," and let Himself die. Jesus let Himself be arrested and let the chief priests beat (Isaiah 50:6; smite meaning: hit with the intent to kill) Him. Jesus let Pilate order Him to be whipped and crucified. Jesus let the soldiers whip Him and let the soldiers put the crown of thorns on His head. Jesus let the soldiers smite Him, spit on His face, and pull out His beard. Jesus let the soldiers nail Him to the cross, and Jesus let Himself die on the cross. Jesus willingly let all of this happen to Himself, thought of you, and silently said, "I love you!"

Jesus went through all of this for the world. He went through all of this for us. Jesus went through all of this agonizing pain for you! Jesus was thinking of you the whole time and silently said, "I love you!" Could you do that for someone, knowing that you had to go through all that agonizing pain to save them?

Knowing you could be rescued from the agonizing pain, but if you were rescued, then the person you were trying to save would not be saved? Knowing that the person did not know you or love you? Jesus did that for you.

Jesus' actions spoke loud and silently said, "I love you!" Would you be able to watch your son or daughter go through all of that agonizing pain for someone else? Knowing you could stop it? God did, and in a very loud way, He silently said, "I love you!" Notice in verse 35 of John 19 that a Roman soldier who was not a believer realized Jesus was telling the truth once he speared Him. He said, "He was telling the truth." Think about it: an unbeliever started to believe in Jesus before He was raised from the dead. Awesome!

John 15:13 (ESV)

[13] Greater love has no one than this, that someone lay down his life for his friends.

"What else must Jesus do to say I love you?" Good question! "You mean there is more?" Yes!

Ephesians 4:8–10 (ESV)

[8] Therefore it says, "When he ascended on high he led a host of captives, and he gave gifts to men."

[9] (In saying, "He ascended," what does it mean but that he had also descended into the lower regions, the earth?

[10] He who descended is the one who also ascended far above all the heavens, that he might fill all things.)

If you will notice in verse 9 it says that Jesus descended into the depths of the lower parts of the earth.

Acts 2:30–31 (ESV)

³⁰ Being therefore a prophet, and knowing that God had sworn with an oath to him that he would set one of his descendants on his throne,

³¹ he foresaw and spoke about the resurrection of the Christ, that he was not abandoned to Hades, nor did his flesh see corruption.

Psalm 16:10 (ESV)

"¹⁰ For you will not abandon my soul to Sheol, or let your holy one see corruption."

All of these verses are talking about Jesus and show that Jesus did go to hell. Notice Jesus would not be left in hell or Hades or among the dead, and His body would not be allowed to rot in the grave.

In Matthew 12:40 (NIV)

Jesus said, "⁴⁰ For as Jonah was three days and three nights in the belly of a huge fish, so the Son of Man will be three days and three nights in the heart of the earth."

Look at what these verses are saying about Jesus. Ephesians 4:9, "Jesus descended into the lower depths, of the earth, (the world)." Acts 2:31, "His soul was not left in hell, in Hades, and among the dead." Psalm 16:10, "God will not leave My (Jesus)

soul in hell, You (God) will not abandon Me to Sheol (which means hell), the place of the dead, You will not leave My soul among the dead." Matthew 12:40, "Shall the Son of man be three days and three nights in the heart of the earth." According to these verses, when Jesus died, He went to hell for three days and three nights in the lower or heart of the earth before He rose from the grave. Jesus did go to hell. The one thing that these verses do not say is whether or not Jesus suffered while He was in hell.

Think about it. What great love Jesus has for you to go through all of what you just read. He did it all for you. What great, incredible, and awesome love that God and Jesus have for you. God loves you. He allowed Jesus to be beaten, whipped, beaten, nailed to the cross, and go to hell just for you. God allowed all of this to happen to Jesus so that you can go to heaven. God loves you so much that He willingly watched His Son go through all that suffering for you. Jesus loves you so much that He willingly went through all that suffering for you. You cannot say God the Father and God the Son (Jesus) have never done anything for you.

Note: If you never read or heard about Jonah and the whale and you want to know what happened, you can find the book of Jonah in the Old Testament of the Bible.

Where is Jesus now?

Acts 2:32–33 (NIV)

[32] God has raised this Jesus to life, and we are all witnesses of it.

³³ Exalted to the right hand of God, he has received from the Father the promised Holy Spirit and has poured out what you now see and hear.

Notice in verse 32 that Luke was writing to those who witnessed the resurrection of Jesus Christ. Jesus was raised from the dead and now sits at the right hand of God. Remember that Jesus, our Lord, our Master, our Savior, and our God took it upon Himself to take the punishment for our sins. He suffered in our place. He paid the price for our sins. God allowed Jesus to take our punishment. Jesus allowed our punishment to happen to Him. God and Jesus did this because They *love you*. Jesus had become the ultimate sacrifice for the world (the people), for me, and for you!

Yes, there are people who gave their lives to save others, but the ones they saved would still eventually die. When anyone else gave their life for others, it was on the spur of the moment. They did not know when they were going to make that sacrifice until that moment. Jesus knew for years that He was going to give His life for everyone and be the ultimate sacrifice. He knew exactly how He was going to die. When Jesus gave His life, He did not die to save our earthly lives. He died to save every single person's spiritual life. Jesus knew He was going to hell for us so that we do not have to go there. What an awesome love He has for us. Jesus Christ loves you!

A side note from Jesus Christ's love for us: When Acts chapter 2 was written, a lot of the eyewitnesses of what was written in the gospels of Jesus were still alive. Note what is said in verse 32, "And we are all witnesses of it." The point is more proof for those who do not believe that this all really did happen.

Luke was writing to people who witnessed everything he was writing about, the people who witnessed the resurrection of Jesus Christ.

There is one more important thing that biblical scholars and pastors will remind me of, and that is that I left out the main part of the cup that Jesus prayed about in Mark 14:36. The verse does not say exactly what the cup of suffering is. Most of us look at it as meaning the physical part of suffering, which was, to Jesus, the minor part of His suffering, according to the Bible. In reading the Bible, we come to know that sin separates us from God and that God cannot stand to look upon sin. Jesus knew that the sin of every single person, past, present, and future, would be on Him, and this would separate Him from God. God the Son would be, and was separated from (Himself), God the Father. This was the main unbearable pain, the cup that Jesus was praying about.

Like any other human being, Jesus did fear physical pain, but what He feared most was being separated from God. Yes, Jesus is God, but He still feared being separated from God the Father. I know it is hard to grasp and understand, but being made sin separated God the Son from Himself, God the Father.

When Jesus said, "My God, my God, why have you forsaken me?" He was quoting Psalm 22:1. Psalm 22 is a conversation of Jesus talking to God about the cup that He was praying about in Mark 14:36. It is very brief on bits and pieces of Jesus acknowledging that God was starting to abandon Him the moment He was arrested and right up to His death on the cross.

2 Corinthians 5:21, KJV

²¹ For he hath made him to be sin for us, who knew no sin; that we might be made the righteousness of God in him.

Yes, I know, I am repeating myself. Jesus, who is God the Son as a human, feared being separated from God the Father, even though it would be for a short period of time. This was the main cup of suffering that Jesus was praying about—being separated from God. This also showed the reality of the human side of Jesus. Jesus, being God at the same time, was human. Wow! What love Jesus has for us, to let Himself become sin itself and be separated from God the Father just for us to be saved.

Romans 5:16–19 (KJV)

¹⁶ (And not as it was by one that sinned, so is the gift: for the judgment was by one to condemnation, but the free gift is of many offences unto justification.

¹⁷ For if by one man's offence death reigned by one; much more they which receive abundance of grace and of the gift of righteousness shall reign in life by one, Jesus Christ.)

¹⁸ Therefore as by the offence of one judgment came upon all men to condemnation; even so by the righteousness of one the free gift came upon all unto justification of life.

¹⁹ For as by one man's disobedience many were made sinners, so by the obedience of one shall many be made righteous.

Adam's disobedience brought death to man. Not just a physical death but a spiritual death. Adam's disobedience caused all men to be made sinners and have judgment and condemnation on them. It separated man from God. Jesus Christ's obedience through His death and resurrection brought justification of life and the free gift of life for men to be made righteous. In 2 Corinthians 5:21, we read Jesus, who knew no sin was made sin so man could be made righteous in Him. Jesus bridged the gap between man and God. It is through Jesus that men are made righteous.

This is for those who can't understand how God could let His own Son be sacrificed for us. After Adam sinned, God initiated animal sacrifice. There had to be the shedding of blood for sin to be forgiven.

Hebrews 9:22 (ESV)

[22] Indeed, under the law almost everything is purified with blood, and without the shedding of blood there is no forgiveness of sins.

Indeed, the shedding of blood did get our sins forgiven, but we still needed a way to go to heaven. "Yes, Mike, but I don't understand why God would let His own Son be sacrificed for us. Why didn't He use or send another human instead of His Son?" Because even though our sin is forgiven, there still had to be a penalty paid for our sins. God knew for us to go to heaven, a perfect human had to be sacrificed and go to hell. God would not have a human suffer for other humans. No human born of man and woman can be perfect. So! He sent His Son (Himself) to become a human, to be that perfect human sacrifice to pay the penalty for our sins. Jesus is the only one who could be totally innocent and is the only one without sin. The shedding of His blood and His taking our place in hell satisfied the penalty of sin once and for all.

Hebrews 10:10 (ESV)

> [10] And by that will we have been sanctified through the offering of the body of Jesus Christ once for all.

Jesus Christ is our God. Jesus Christ loves you so much that He bore the punishment for your sins. He paid the price for you. Jesus Christ willingly let Himself be sacrificed for you. God loves you so much that He had His Son take your punishment for your sins for you. God had Jesus Christ pay the price for you to go to heaven. God let God the Son (let God Himself) be sacrificed for you. God and Jesus love you.

No one, not a single person, can say no one loves them. Even if they feel no one on Earth loves them, God and God the Son, Jesus Christ, love them.

We always look at the biblical aspect that our sins nailed Jesus to the cross. But we never think of or look at the realistic aspect that Jesus had a choice. Otherwise, Jesus would not have prayed for God to take the cup away from Him. Jesus knew there had to be a perfect sacrifice and He was the only one that could be that perfect sacrifice. He had a choice to choose to avoid what He feared or to choose to go through with it. Jesus chose to go through with it and die on the cross to save us because He loves us.

Jesus Christ did the greatest thing for you that no one else could do. He suffered, died on the cross, and went to hell for you so you can be born again and know for sure that you are going to heaven when your body dies. If He did not do this, you would be going to hell. The pain in hell is scrutinizing forever. In John 3:7, Jesus said, "You must be born again." "Born again" is explained completely in chapter 6.

CHAPTER 5:

WHAT HAPPENED TO JESUS' BODY WHILE HIS SPIRIT WAS IN HELL, AND WHAT HAPPENED WHEN HE ROSE FROM THE DEAD?

Before I start on the subjects of this chapter, I have to make some statements. Biblical scholars say the following verses in Matthew have some gray areas of doctrinal beliefs. Matthew is the only one who gives an account of an earthquake happening the moment Jesus died and when He rose from the dead. Matthew is the only one who gives an account of many godly dead coming out of the graves after Jesus' resurrection. Matthew is the only one who gives an account of the curtain or veil that was in the tabernacle of Jerusalem being torn in two. Biblical scholars are skeptical of these accounts as to whether or not they happened because Matthew is the only one who recorded these four events. Yet, Matthew was inspired by God to write what he wrote.

The thing that biblical scholars are most skeptical about is what happened to the godly men and women who were raised from the dead because the Bible does not say what happened to them or why God raised them from the dead. We can only speculate what the answers may be. I can only give you a possibility of why and where they may have gone.

Note: One needs to pay attention to all the words in a verse. The word "after" plays a big part in when the godly dead were raised from the grave in Matthew 27:53.

One would think that one should or may believe these accounts because of what 2 Timothy 3:16 says, "All Scripture is given by inspiration of God and is profitable for doctrine, for reproof, for correction, for instruction in righteousness." These accounts in Matthew are Scriptures that were given by inspiration of God. I purposely pointed out these facts because scholars have skepticism and speculations on these accounts. As I talk about these accounts, I am also speculating on whether the godly dead went to heaven or not after these events took place. However, the rest of the things in this chapter I am not speculating about but rather stating the facts of what happened based on what is written in the Bible.

While Jesus' Spirit was in hell, we have to look at what happened to His body here on Earth and at the events that took place to prove His body was not stolen and that He did rise from the dead. "So, Mike, what happened to Jesus' body while His Spirit was in hell?" First, let's look at what happened when Jesus died on the cross. Believe me, when anyone else died, the following things have never happened just because they died.

Matthew 27:50–54 (NIV)

[50] And when Jesus had cried out again in a loud voice, he gave up his spirit.

> ⁵¹ At that moment the curtain of the temple was torn in two from top to bottom. The earth shook, the rocks split
>
> ⁵² and the tombs broke open. The bodies of many holy people who had died were raised to life.
>
> ⁵³ They came out of the tombs after Jesus' resurrection and went into the holy city and appeared to many people.
>
> ⁵⁴ When the centurion and those with him who were guarding Jesus saw the earthquake and all that had happened, they were terrified, and exclaimed, "Surely he was the Son of God!"

What did Jesus cry out just before He died? As we read in John 19:30, He said, "It is finished." Then He let Himself die by giving up His own Spirit. Right when Jesus died, at that moment, the curtain in the temple of Jerusalem was torn in two from the top to the bottom. Then came an earthquake that shook the earth and split the rocks. The Roman officer and the other Roman soldiers were not believers, nor were they Jews, yet they were saying, "This man truly was the Son of God!" That is amazing. Because of what just happened, the Roman soldiers believed.

Now, back to your question. "What happened to Jesus' body while His Spirit was in hell?" Jesus' Spirit went to hell. Meanwhile, back at the ranch, what happened to His body? Starting with the evening of the day that Jesus died, let's go back to the book of Matthew.

Chapter 5: What Happened to Jesus' Body...?

> Matthew 27:57-60 (NIV)
>
> [57] As evening approached, there came a rich man from Arimathea, named Joseph, who had himself become a disciple of Jesus.
>
> [58] Going to Pilate, he asked for Jesus' body, and Pilate ordered that it be given to him.
>
> [59] Joseph took the body, wrapped it in a clean linen cloth,
>
> [60] and placed it in his own new tomb that he had cut out of the rock. He rolled a big stone in front of the entrance to the tomb and went away.

After Jesus died, His body was given to a rich man named Joseph, who had become a disciple of Jesus (he was not one of the twelve). He wrapped Jesus' body in a clean linen cloth, put it in a tomb carved out of rock, and closed the entrance with a large stone. The following verses are so clear about what happens next that they do not need any explanation (again, this is about what happened to Jesus' body back at the ranch while His Spirit was in hell). Let's read on,

> Matthew 27:61-66 (NIV)
>
> [61] Mary Magdalene and the other Mary were sitting there opposite the tomb.
>
> [62] The next day, the one after Preparation Day, the chief priests and the Pharisees went to Pilate.

⁶³ "Sir," they said, "we remember that while he was still alive that deceiver said, 'After three days I will rise again.'

⁶⁴ So give the order for the tomb to be made secure until the third day. Otherwise, his disciples may come and steal the body and tell the people that he has been raised from the dead. This last deception will be worse than the first."

⁶⁵ "Take a guard," Pilate answered, "Go, make the tomb as secure as you know how."

⁶⁶ So they went and made the tomb secure by putting a seal on the stone and posting the guard.

Now, because of how much the chief priests and the Pharisees did not want the people to believe that Jesus would rise from the dead, I have no doubt in my mind that they kept an eye on Jesus' body from the moment that He died. The chief priests and the Pharisees wanted to make sure there was no way that anyone could prove that Jesus Christ rose from the dead. I think they kept an eye on Joseph as he took Jesus' body, wrapped it, and laid it in the tomb. They were so afraid of it being said that Jesus had been raised from the dead that they did not let Jesus' body or His tomb out of their sight until after the whole three days had gone by. This way, they could definitely say, "Jesus, this deceiver, did not rise from the dead."

Chapter 5: What Happened to Jesus' Body...?

Matthew 28:1-6 (NIV)

¹ After the Sabbath, at dawn on the first day of the week, Mary Magdalene and the other Mary went to look at the tomb.

² There was a violent earthquake, for an angel of the Lord came down from heaven and, going to the tomb, rolled back the stone and sat on it.

³ His appearance was like lightning, and his clothes were white as snow.

⁴ The guards were so afraid of him that they shook and became like dead men.

⁵ The angel said to the women, "Do not be afraid, for I know that you are looking for Jesus, who was crucified.

⁶ He is not here; he has risen, just as he said. Come and see the place where he lay."

Acts 26:23 (NIV)

"²³ That the Messiah would suffer and, as the first to rise from the dead, would bring the message of light to his own people and to the Gentiles."

Colossians 1:18 (NIV)

"¹⁸ And he is the head of the body, the church; he is the beginning and the firstborn from among the dead, so that in everything he might have the supremacy."

Revelation 1:5 (NIV)

"⁵ And from Jesus Christ, who is the faithful witness, the firstborn from the dead, and the ruler of the kings of the earth."

We need to keep in mind all the verses we just read as I explain them to help you understand the facts that I am stating.

Note: In the Bible, there were some people like Lazarus in John 11:32-44 who were raised from the dead. They were raised to live and walk on Earth once again for another time to die. Jesus was the first to rise from the dead to go to heaven. The Bible does not say that those who were raised from the dead before Jesus were born from the dead but just raised from the dead. There is a difference. Jesus was not the first to have ever been raised from the dead but He is the first born from the dead.

The verses we just read show Jesus was the firstborn from the dead and the first to be resurrected from the dead to go to heaven. If you will note, God had Matthew use the word "after," which tells us after Jesus' resurrection is when "the tombs opened, and the bodies of many godly men and women who had died were raised from the dead, and they went into the holy city of Jerusalem, and appeared to many people." They were raised from the dead not to die again but to go to heaven. The reason why Jesus Christ was raised first to go to heaven is that, without His resurrection, the others would not have been able to be resurrected to go to heaven.

Matthew said many were raised from the dead. I do not think they had just died like Lazarus before he was raised from the dead. They most likely had been dead for a while because the number was many, not just a few, and they were only godly men and women.

Matthew is very clear in verse 27:51, "The earth shook, the rocks split." According to Matthew, an earthquake took place right after the moment that Jesus died. "The earth shook, the rocks split." Then, in Matthew 28:2, a second earthquake took place, which was a great, violent earthquake because Jesus had risen from the dead. During the second earthquake in Matthew 28:2, when Matthew 27:52-53 took place, the tombs and graves opened up, and many of the godly dead came out and walked into Jerusalem and appeared before many people, for Jesus had risen.

"An angel of the Lord came down from heaven and, going to the tomb, rolled back the stone and sat on it." The angel rolled the stone away, not to let Jesus out but to let the people in to see that Jesus was not there. The quake took place to let the godly men and women come out of their graves and tombs. I believe both earthquakes did happen. I believe the Bible because God wrote it. I believe the dead did come out of the graves during the earthquake in Matthew 28:2. "Why?" That is definitely a good question. Matthew 27:52-53 says the dead came out of the graves after Jesus' resurrection. The key words here are "after Jesus' resurrection." They came out of the graves after His resurrection.

The guards were so afraid that they became like dead men. They were not dead, but they could not move because of their fear. What took place in Matthew 27:52-53 is the only time in the Bible where many dead came up out of the grave because of someone dying and then rising from the dead. The people that rose from the dead did not walk like zombies; they were alive like you and me. Matthew did not say why those from the graves appeared to the many people in the holy city of Jerusalem. Maybe they knew them; we don't know. But this, too, was or could have been a testimony that Jesus Christ had risen from the dead.

Remember, the Jewish leaders did not want the people to believe that Jesus was raised from the dead. That might be why these events are not recorded in Jewish historical history.

I want you to notice two things in Matthew 27:52–53; the first is that it was after Jesus' resurrection when "the bodies of many godly men and women who had died were raised from the dead. They left the cemetery and went into the holy city of Jerusalem." The second thing is they all were godly men and women.

Note: People in the Bible that were raised from the dead before Jesus was arrested and died on the cross walked and lived on Earth only to die and go back to the grave again. They were not born from the dead to go to heaven; they were just raised from the dead to live on Earth once again. If this note is not true, then Jesus cannot be the firstborn from the dead.

Those who were raised from the dead in verses 52–53 did not die again; they were born from the dead to go to heaven. Why else would God raise them from the dead? I believe the godly dead came out of the graves during the second earthquake in Matthew 28:2 because of what verse 53 says, "They came out of the graves after his resurrection."

I am not done yet; there is more. Now go back and read Acts 26:23, Colossians 1:18, and Revelation 1:5 again. These verses say Jesus is the firstborn from the dead. "Why is Jesus the firstborn from the dead?" Bear with me as I answer your question.

Those who were forgiven and died before Jesus did could not go to heaven because there was no way for anyone to go to heaven until Jesus died on the cross, rose from the dead, and went to heaven Himself.

Jesus had to be resurrected first in order for anyone who died physically *before* Him could go to heaven. The significance of Jesus' resurrection is what made Him the firstborn from the dead. This way those who were saved but in the grave could go to heaven. Verses 52–53 happened after Jesus' resurrection.

For the sake of the scholars, still speculating, here are some of the main reasons why I believe that what happened in Matthew 27:52-53 took place during and after the second earthquake in Matthew 28:2.

These verses are the inspired Word of God. Those who were raised from the dead before Jesus were not born from the dead to go to heaven but just raised from the dead to live and die again. They were not dead for very long and did not go to heaven after they were raised from the dead. According to the Scriptures, Jesus is the firstborn from the dead who went to heaven. The godly men and women did not just die; they most likely were dead for a while because there were many of them. One would think the only reason why God would raise only godly people is for them to go to heaven because when He raised them, it was after Jesus' resurrection. I rest my case. Now, having said all of that, let us move on.

Read the rest of Matthew and see how Jesus had visited His disciples and they worshipped Him. How the chief priests and elders gave the soldiers large sums of money to break the law (the commandment, "You shall not lie") for them to lie about Jesus' resurrection. The chief priest told the soldiers to say that they had fallen asleep and that someone had stolen Jesus' body while they were asleep. Think about it: if any of the Jewish leaders had stolen Jesus' body, they would have said, "Look, we have Jesus' body. He did not rise from the dead." As you read the Bible, you will see that the disciples went into hiding for fear of their own lives. They were too scared to even think of stealing Jesus' body.

When you read the last verses of the other Gospels of Mark, Luke, and John, Jesus was taken up into heaven and seated at the right hand of God.

Did all of what we read about Jesus really happen? Yes! Let us read from a man who once persecuted the church. He would track down the followers of Jesus Christ and arrest them so that they could be tried and sentenced to death. He had no mercy for those who believed and followed Jesus. Now, he testifies of the one that he himself once did not believe in. His name is Paul. Here is just a little of what God had the apostle Paul write.

1 Corinthians 15:1–11 (NIV)

¹ Now, brothers and sisters, I want to remind you of the gospel I preached to you, which you received and on which you have taken your stand.

² By this gospel you are saved, if you hold firmly to the word I preached to you. Otherwise, you have believed in vain.

³ For what I received I passed on to you as of first importance: that Christ died for our sins according to the Scriptures,

⁴ that he was buried, that he was raised on the third day according to the Scriptures,

⁵ and that he appeared to Cephas, and then to the Twelve.

⁶ After that, he appeared to more than five hundred of the brothers and sisters at the same time, most of whom are still living, though some have fallen asleep.

⁷ Then he appeared to James, then to all the apostles,

⁸ and last of all he appeared to me also, as to one abnormally born.

⁹ For I am the least of the apostles and do not even deserve to be called an apostle, because I persecuted the church of God.

¹⁰ But by the grace of God I am what I am, and his grace to me was not without effect. No, I worked harder than all of them—yet not I, but the grace of God that was with me.

¹¹ Whether, then, it is I or they, this is what we preach, and this is what you believed.

Paul goes on to preach a great message in the rest of 1 Corinthians chapter 15, but I want to point out some other things in these first eleven verses. Paul, a man who did not believe in Jesus and went after believers to have them put to death, was changed. Paul was 100 percent against Jesus. Paul was just like the Jewish leader who wanted to put an end to the following of this deceiver, Jesus Christ. Now, Paul knows that Jesus is the Son of God. Now not only does he believe, but he is preaching

God's Word about Jesus. Paul is telling us that Christ died for our sins according to the Scriptures, that He was buried, and that He was raised on the third day according to the Scriptures. When Paul said the Scriptures, he was referring to the Old Testament, which was called the Scriptures in that time period.

Paul is saying to us that the Scriptures have been fulfilled. Paul is writing this letter to the Corinthian church. Most of them were alive when Jesus appeared to over five hundred people at one time after His resurrection. They knew Paul was telling the truth because they were witnesses to what Paul was saying. Paul was writing to those who were a part of that five hundred. The strong point I want to bring out is that no one stole Jesus' body from the tomb. They saw Jesus and talked with Jesus after He died on the cross and rose from the dead.

Jesus had appeared to a lot of people. To top it off, He appeared to over five hundred people at one time. Back in Jesus' time, women and children were not considered important enough to count when a large number of people were counted. When we read that Jesus appeared to over five hundred people, that number most likely did not include the women and children. I am only speculating, but at that time it may have been over a thousand people with the women and children. One of the reasons why Jesus appeared to all the people He did was to prove that He did rise up from the dead.

In my research for the size of the curtain that was torn in two when Jesus died, I found that the size of the curtain is not in the Bible. We are told in the Bible what the curtain is made out of.

Exodus 26:31–35 (NIV)

³¹ Make a curtain of blue, purple and scarlet yarn and finely twisted linen, with cherubim worked into it by a skilled worker.

³² Hang it with gold hooks on four posts of acacia wood overlaid with gold and standing on four silver bases.

³³ Hang the curtain from the clasps and place the ark of the covenant law behind the curtain. The curtain will separate the Holy Place from the Most Holy Place.

³⁴ Put the atonement cover on the ark of the covenant law in the Most Holy Place.

³⁵ Place the table outside the curtain on the north side of the tabernacle and put the lampstand opposite it on the south side.

I am not concerned whether it is the north or south where they placed the two items in the tabernacle. I wanted you to see how the temple veil or curtain was constructed. By the description of the curtain and where it was placed, it must have looked beautiful.

Because of scholars' research on the history of the building of the Jewish temple and the making of the curtain, I found out the size of the curtain. The curtain that was torn in two when Jesus died was sixty feet in height, thirty feet in width, and four inches thick. One was made every two years for the temple. It is said that the curtain could not be torn by an earthquake or by falling. The curtain was so heavy it took at least 300 priests to move the curtain. This curtain could not be destroyed or torn by hand. This curtain was torn in two from top to bottom the moment that Jesus died on the cross. Only God could have torn the curtain in half.

"Mike, what is the significance of this curtain or veil being torn in two?" I do not want to go into depth about it, but here is a part of why the veil was torn. Only the Jewish high priest could go beyond the curtain, which was the Holy of Holies in the temple, to be in the presence of God. The people had to go to the high priest to get to God.

Sin separates us from God. Jesus' atonement for our sins tore down the wall of separation between God and man so that everyone is now able to come into the place of holiness, the presence of God. Therefore, the veil is no longer necessary.

Remember all that Jesus Christ did for you. Remember how much God the Father and God the Son (Jesus) love you. Jesus' actions spoke louder than words, and He silently said, "I love you!"

The chief priests, the Pharisees, the Sadducees, the elders, and the high council of the Jewish leaders of Jesus' time did not believe that Jesus was the Messiah, the Son of God. They wanted to make sure that no one would steal His body from the grave and say that He rose from the dead. If this had happened, then they would have had a bigger problem because more people would start to believe in Jesus and follow Him. Every time that the chief priests tried to show Jesus to be wrong, they failed. Now that Jesus was dead, they did not want to fail again in proving that Jesus was wrong and that He was a deceiver. But they did fail because there was nothing they could do to stop Jesus' resurrection from the dead. The chief priests, the Pharisees, and the Sadducees definitely wanted to put an end to the following of this deceiver. They went through a lot of trouble to prove that Jesus did not rise from the dead. They wanted the people to stop believing in Jesus so badly that they even went as far as to break two of God's commandments. The first was to find false witnesses against Jesus. The second was to give large sums of money to the soldiers who guarded Jesus' tomb to lie. To say that they fell asleep and that someone stole Jesus' body while they were sleeping. In reading the four Gospels, occasionally, the Jewish leaders would accuse Jesus of breaking their laws; then, they tried to disprove Jesus by breaking their laws themselves.

Back then, Roman soldiers would be put to death if they fell asleep on guard duty. They did not fall asleep. If Jesus' body had been stolen, the Jewish leaders of that time would have known and got a hold of it to display it in public. They would have said, "Look, Jesus did not rise from the dead. He deceived all of you." It would have been a lot easier to prove that Jesus did not rise from the dead and that He was not who He said He was if His body had been stolen.

The proof is in the pudding: Jesus' body was not stolen, and Jesus did rise from the dead. With all of the written testimonies of Jesus Christ appearing to so many people after He died on the cross, how can we say He did not rise from the dead? We can't. My main point about what happened to Jesus' body is that it was not stolen. We have a risen Savior!

CHAPTER 6:

Why Did Jesus Have to Suffer, And What It Means to Be Born Again

"Why did Jesus have to go through all that suffering for us?" Jesus had to suffer so we would have a way to go to heaven. There had to be a high price paid for our sins, and Jesus' death was that price. "Do you mean there is no other way to go to heaven?" Yes, that is correct. If Jesus had not shed His blood for us through the beatings, the whipping, dying on the cross, going to hell, and rising from the dead, we would not have a way to go to heaven.

For a better understanding of why Jesus had to suffer, I must repeat some of the things I have said. After Adam sinned, God initiated animal sacrifice. There had to be the shedding of blood for sin to be forgiven. The book of Leviticus talks about the sacrificing of animals and sprinkling (shedding) of their blood on the altar. It talks about how the blood of any creature is life. It talks about the high priest sacrificing animals and sprinkling (shedding) their blood to make atonement for a person's sins to be forgiven. This was done once a year (read Exodus 30:10 and Hebrews 9:7).

But this did not get us into heaven. Because there still had to be a penalty paid for our sins. God knew in order for us to go to heaven, a perfect human had to be sacrificed. God would not have a human suffer for other humans. No human born of man and woman can be perfect. So! He sent His Son (Himself) to become a human, to be that perfect human sacrifice to pay the penalty for our sins. Jesus was totally innocent and was the only one without sin. He was the final sacrifice. The shedding of His blood satisfied the penalty of sin once and for all.

> Leviticus 16:30 (ESV)
>
> [30] For on this day shall atonement be made for you to cleanse you. You shall be clean before the LORD from all your sins.

> Hebrews 9:22 (ESV)
>
> [22] Indeed, under the law almost everything is purified with blood, and without the shedding of blood there is no forgiveness of sins.

Under the law, without the shedding of blood, there is no remission or forgiveness of sins.

> Hebrews 10:10 (ESV)
>
> [10] And by that will we have been sanctified through the offering of the body of Jesus Christ once for all.

Jesus Christ is our God. He bore the punishment for your sins for you. He paid the price for you. Through the offering of Jesus Christ's body, we are sanctified, made clean before the LORD from all of our sins.

God said in Jeremiah 33:8 (ESV)

⁸ I will cleanse them from all the guilt of their sin against me, and I will forgive all the guilt of their sin and rebellion against me.

Romans 5:8-9 (ESV)

⁸ But God shows his love for us in that while we were still sinners, Christ died for us.

⁹ Since, therefore, we have now been justified by his blood, much more shall we be saved by him from the wrath of God.

In verse 9, we are told that we are now justified by Jesus' blood, and we are saved from the wrath of God through Jesus.

Hebrews 9:12-14 (ESV)

¹² He entered once for all into the holy places, not by means of the blood of goats and calves but by means of his own blood, thus securing an eternal redemption.

¹³ For if the blood of goats and bulls, and the sprinkling of defiled persons with the ashes of a heifer, sanctify for the purification of the flesh,

¹⁴ how much more will the blood of Christ, who through the eternal Spirit offered himself without blemish to God, purify our conscience from dead works to serve the living God.

Hebrews 10:3–4 (ESV)

³ But in these sacrifices there is a reminder of sins every year. ⁴ For it is impossible for the blood of bulls and goats to take away sins.

In reading these verses we can clearly see that animal sacrifices and the shedding of their blood could only get our sins forgiven. Their blood does not save us from God's wrath, does not take away our sins, and does not secure eternal redemption for us. Our salvation from God's wrath could only be obtained by the blood of Jesus Christ.

Romans 5:16–19 (KJV)

¹⁶ (And not as it was by one that sinned, so is the gift: for the judgment was by one to condemnation, but the free gift is of many offences unto justification.

¹⁷ For if by one man's offence death reigned by one; much more they which receive abundance of grace and of the gift of righteousness shall reign in life by one, Jesus Christ.)

¹⁸ Therefore as by the offence of one judgment came upon all men to condemnation; even so by the righteousness of one the free gift came upon all unto justification of life.

¹⁹ For as by one man's disobedience many were made sinners, so by the obedience of one shall many be made righteous.

This paragraph is worth repeating. Adam's disobedience brought death to man. Not just a physical death but a spiritual death. Adam's disobedience caused all men to be made sinners and have judgment and condemnation on them. It separated man from God. Jesus Christ's obedience through His death and resurrection brought justification of life and the free gift of life for men to be made righteous. In 2 Corinthians 5:21, we read Jesus, "Who knew no sin was made to be sin so man could be made righteous in Him." Jesus bridged the gap between man and God. It is through Jesus that men are made righteous.

John 14:6 (NIV)

⁶ Jesus answered, "I am the way and the truth and the life. No one comes to the Father except through me."

Jesus makes it very clear in what He is saying. He is saying that He is the only way, the only truth, and the only life. No one, nobody, but nobody can come to God except through Him. Jesus is the only way to get to God, the only truth to get to God, and the only life to get to God. There is no other way, truth, or life to get to God. We have to go through Jesus. He did not say, "I am one of the ways to come to God." He said, "I am the way and the truth and the life. No one comes to the Father except through me."

Acts 4:11–12 (ESV)

¹¹ This Jesus is the stone that was rejected by you, the builders, which has become the cornerstone.

¹² And there is salvation in no one else, for there is no other name under heaven given among men by which we must be saved.

Again we see that the only way that we can be saved is by Jesus. There is no other way to get saved (Acts 11:12); there is no salvation in anyone else. Jesus is the only one who can save us. Yes! We are to be a good person, but just being a good person will not save us. Isaiah 64:6a (KJV), "6 But we are all as an unclean thing, and all our righteousness are as filthy rags." Jesus is the only way to God and the only way to heaven. We are to repent of our sins and ask Jesus Christ for the forgiveness of our sins. Jesus gave His life to free us from our sins and from a spiritual death.

No one can get to heaven without Jesus. Jesus took our punishment for our disobedience to God. Jesus is the only way of salvation.

Acts 16:30–33 (NIV)

³⁰ He then brought them out and asked, "Sirs, what must I do to be saved?"

³¹ They replied, "Believe in the Lord Jesus, and you will be saved—you and your household."

³² Then they spoke the word of the Lord to him and to all the others in his house.

³³ At that hour of the night the jailer took them and washed their wounds; then immediately he and all his family were baptized.

There is a lot going on in Acts 16:30-33, but there are only two things that I want to point out. In verse 31, they said, "Believe in the Lord Jesus, and you will be saved." This statement is saying when you believe in the Lord Jesus, you will be saved. Can a newborn baby believe in the Lord Jesus? No. First, we are saved, and then we are baptized. After they believed (got saved), then they were baptized. Their baptism did not save them. My point is they did not say, "Get baptized, and you will be saved." Yes, they did get baptized, but not until after believing in the Lord Jesus to be saved.

Take note of the answer they were given when they asked, "What must I do to be saved?" They answered, "Believe on the Lord Jesus Christ, and thou shall be saved, and thy house" (KJV). In the AMP, "And they answered, Believe in the Lord Jesus Christ [give yourself up to Him, take yourself out of your own keeping and entrust yourself into His keeping] and you will be saved, [and this applies both to] you and your household as well."

Ephesians 2:8 (NIV)

⁸ For it is by grace you have been saved, through faith—and this is not from yourselves [you can't take credit for this], it is a gift from God.

It said, "By grace, you are saved; it is the gift of God." What is God's gift to us? Jesus Christ, "God gave us His only begotten Son," as we read in John 3:16. Grace is unmerited favor. If you are not saved, we will get to that before the end of this chapter. Right now let us look at who is our high priest according to what the Bible says.

Hebrews 7:26–28, 8:1–2 (NIV)

²⁶ Such a high priest truly meets our need—one who is holy, blameless, pure, set apart from sinners, exalted above the heavens.

²⁷ Unlike the other high priests, he does not need to offer sacrifices day after day, first for his own sins, and then for the sins of the people. He sacrificed for their sins once for all when he offered himself.

²⁸ For the law appoints as high priests men in all their weakness; but the oath, which came after the law, appointed the Son, who has been made perfect forever.

¹ Now the main point of what we are saying is this: We do have such a high priest, who sat down at the right hand of the throne of the Majesty in heaven,

² and who serves in the sanctuary, the true tabernacle set up by the Lord, not by a mere human being.

These verses describe and talk about Jesus, about one of the many things Jesus is to us. Jesus Christ is the only human sacrifice that God has ever received for our (your) sins. When you accepted Jesus as your personal Savior, He became your high priest. God has appointed and made Jesus Christ our High Priest. Jesus Christ does not have to ask for forgiveness of His sins because He has never sinned. Jesus is now our one and only High Priest. Jesus is the one that you have to ask for the forgiveness of your sins. If you truly repent of your sins (strive to live your life without sin, turn away from your sins), God and Jesus will forgive you of your sins. In order for Jesus Christ to have been able to die on the cross for us, He had to be without sin in His life. Jesus never committed a sin. He is our high priest.

> 2 Corinthians 5:21 (ESV)
>
> [21] For our sake he made him to be sin who knew no sin, so that in him we might become the righteousness of God.

If Jesus Christ had committed just one sin, He would not have been able to die on the cross for us. Jesus was made sin so we could be made righteous and have a relationship with God.

When the high priest would offer up an animal for the sins of the people, their sins were forgiven, but they still were not going to heaven. When Jesus Christ became the ultimate sacrifice, not only were our sins forgiven, but now we have a way to go to heaven. Before Jesus Christ died on the cross, there was no way to go to heaven.

"So! Now that we know there is a way to go to heaven, how do we know for sure that we are going to heaven when we die?" I am so glad that you asked that question. I am going to answer that question and also tell you what God expects of us after we become born again. There is a lot to learn and to understand about what God expects of you, and that is what God and I are going to help you with.

> Matthew 18:2-4 (AMP)
>
> [2] And He called a little child to Himself and put him in the midst of them,

> ³ And said, Truly I say to you, unless you repent (change, turn about) and become like little children [trusting, lowly, loving, forgiving], you can never enter the kingdom of heaven [at all].
>
> ⁴ Whoever will humble himself therefore and become like this little child [trusting, lowly, loving, forgiving] is greatest in the kingdom of heaven.

Jesus said in Mark 10:15 (NIV)

> "¹⁵ Truly I tell you, anyone who will not receive the kingdom of God like a little child will never enter it."

Jesus did not say that unless you are baptized, you cannot enter the kingdom of God.

Jesus said that unless you repent and be as humble as a little child, you cannot enter the kingdom of God. A little child trusts and believes their parents with all their heart. This is how God wants you to come to Him, to trust and believe in Him completely with all your heart. When you read God's Word, God wants you to believe what is written. God also wants you to trust Him. Just as you believed in and trusted in your parents when you were little, that is what God wants you to do with Him. You must come to God as a little child, trusting Him and believing in Him completely, with all your heart.

A side note: Unfortunately, not everyone has loving parents, so it is harder for them to come to God as little children, believing and trusting in Him, because they could not do that with their own parents. God is love, and He is not like unloving earthly parents.

"Well, now! Because Jesus is the only way to heaven, and He died for the world (everybody), then everyone is going to heaven, right?" No, that is wrong. Unfortunately, not everybody is going to heaven. Yes, Jesus did die on the cross for every last one of us, but in order for every person to go to heaven, each person has to receive Jesus as their personal Savior. But not everyone will or has received Jesus Christ as their personal Savior because they choose not to. Therefore, not every single one of us is going to heaven. Please read on, and you will know why I wrote these statements.

Jesus said in Matthew 7:21–23

(AMP), "²¹ Not everyone who says to Me, Lord, Lord, will enter the kingdom of heaven, but he who does the will of My Father Who is in heaven.

²² Many will say to Me on that day, Lord, Lord, have we not prophesied in Your name and driven out demons in Your name and done many mighty works in Your name?

²³ And then I will say to them openly (publicly), I never knew you; depart from Me, you who act wickedly [disregarding My commands]."

(NIV), "²¹ Not everyone who says to me, 'Lord, Lord,' will enter the kingdom of heaven, but only he who [actually] does the will of my Father who is in heaven [will enter]."

²² Many will say to me on that day, 'Lord, Lord, did we not prophesy in your name, and in your name

drive out demons and in your name performed many miracles?'

²³ Then I will tell them plainly, 'I never knew you. Away from me, you evildoers!' "

Jesus was talking to believers about what will happen on judgment day. They may have cast out demons, prophesied in His name, and performed many miracles in His name, but in their personal lives, they were not doers of God's will, which is His Word, the Bible. He would not have said all of this if everyone was going to heaven. According to what Jesus said in Matthew, we can conclude that not only do we have to be born again, but we also have to be doers of His Word in order to go to heaven.

James 2:20 (NIV)

²⁰ You foolish person, do you want evidence that faith without deeds is useless?

Romans 2:13 (NIV)

¹³ For it is not those who hear the law who are righteous in God's sight, but it is those who obey the law who will be declared righteous.

In James' question we can see that faith without good works is useless and dead. Not only do we have to believe, have faith, and be born again, but to make our faith worthy and alive, we need to do good works. Once we are born again, the Holy Spirit gives us the desire to be obedient to God and helps us to be doers of the Word.

In the Gospel of John, Jesus said that we must be "born again."

John 3:3, 5-7 (NIV)

³ Jesus replied, "Very truly I tell you, no one can see the kingdom of God unless they are born again."

⁵ ...Jesus answered, "Very truly I tell you, no one can enter the kingdom of God unless they are born of water and the Spirit.

⁶ Flesh gives birth to flesh, but the Spirit [the Holy Spirit] gives birth to [spiritual life] spirit.

⁷ You should not be surprised at my saying, 'You must be born again.'"

As you can see, you must be born again to get into God's kingdom. "What does 'born again' mean?" That is what we are going to learn and understand next. What "born again" means according to the Bible, not according to a church or a religious belief. Being "born again" is not being of a religion, being religious, being holier than thou, or acting holier than thou. Being "born again" is a spiritual birth according to God's Word. It is not a religious act. "Well then, what is 'born again'?" Being "born again" is a way of life, living for God. The following will explain what Jesus meant by saying "born again."

John 1:12-13 (NIV)

¹² Yet to all who received him, to those who believed in his name, he gave the right to become children of God—

¹³ children born not of natural descent, nor of human decision or a husband's will, but born of God.

Notice that in verse 12, John is talking about all who believed and accepted Jesus; he said nothing about being baptized. In verse 13, John is speaking of those who are born spiritually. John is saying, "To all who believed Him and accepted Him" are those who are born spiritually. We have to receive Him.

This is what being born again means. Here are some words to better understand these two verses, along with the verse John 3:6, "What is born of physical flesh is a physical birth," which is being born from your parents. "What is born of the Holy Spirit is a spiritual birth," born of God by receiving Jesus Christ as your personal Savior, your spirit now comes to life. First, you are born alive physically, your first birth, then when you receive Jesus Christ as your personal Savior, you have your second birth. Your spirit, which was dead at your physical (first) birth, now becomes alive through Jesus Christ, which is your second birth.

Let's look at more Scriptures to show why I say we are born with a dead spirit.

Ephesians 2:1–5 (NIV)

¹ As for you, you were dead in your transgression and sins,

² in which you used to live when you followed the ways of this world and of the ruler of the kingdom of the air, the spirit who is now at work in those who are disobedient [to God].

> ³ All of us also live among them at one time, gratifying the cravings of our flesh and following its desires and thoughts. Like the rest, we were by nature deserving of wrath.
>
> ⁴ But because of his great love for us, God, who is rich in mercy,
>
> ⁵ made us alive with Christ even when we were dead in transgressions—it is by grace you have been saved.

These verses say a lot, but right now, I only want to point out two of the things that they are saying. This is to help you understand more of what it means to be born again. Remember, earlier, we talked about a spiritual birth. Well, as you can see, these verses show us that God considers us spiritually dead while we are willfully sinning against Him. "You were dead because of your sins." When we were willfully living a life of sin, God said that our spirit was dead.

Note: This means even the smallest of sins. Even though our bodies are alive, our spirits are dead because of our sins. When your spirit is born, this is your second birth, what Jesus calls being born again. "You must be born again to see and to enter the kingdom of God." Jesus did not say you must be baptized to enter the kingdom of God. This will also help those who are told to say, "Yes, I have been baptized," when asked, "Are you born again?" You are not saved by your baptism, according to the Bible. Yes, we will get to the verse that says, "Baptism does also now save us." That is not the whole verse in the Bible. I will explain what that whole verse means later in chapter 7.

Notice that in verse 1, Paul said you were dead in your trespasses and sins. Were you physically dead while you were committing trespasses and sins? No, but verse 1 says once you were dead. "We know that we are physically alive when we are committing trespasses and sins, so why does it say we were dead?" Because it is our spirit that was dead, not our bodies. Read Ephesians 2:1–5 again; our spirit was dead, and now it is alive.

"Mike, why do you say that we have to receive Jesus Christ as our personal Savior?" That is a good question.

Ephesians 2:8–9 (NIV)

⁸ For it is by grace you have been saved, through faith—and this is not from yourselves [you can't take credit for this], it is the gift of God—

⁹ not by works [a reward for the good things we have done], so that no one can boast [about it].

It is by the grace (which means God's unmerited favor and mercy, which we do not deserve) of God that you are saved. Salvation is a gift from God. God gave it to the world, to you and me. Through Jesus Christ's suffering, death, shed blood, and resurrection is God's gift of unmerited love for you (us). He gave this free gift of salvation so no man can boast, which means brag, so no man can brag of his salvation. It is through this gift that you have eternal life in that you will go to heaven. Jesus is that gift to us from God. As we read earlier in John 3:16, to paraphrase, God loved the world so much that He gave His one and only Son so that everyone who believes (believes meaning: trusts in, clings to, relies on, and receives Him) in Him will not perish but have eternal life.

"But Mike, I believe in Jesus and in God; I am a good person. I do not do sinful things. Why do I have to receive Jesus to go to heaven?" John 1:12, "To those who receive and accept him (Jesus)," are given the right to become children of God.

The demons believe in Jesus and God, and they are not going to heaven.

James 2:19 (NIV)

¹⁹ You believe that there is one God. Good! Even the demons believe that—and shudder.

To believe is not enough, you have to receive. "Even the demons believe, and they tremble in terror." "Even the demons believe and shudder." Why do demons believe and tremble or shudder? Because even though they believe, they know they are not going to heaven but to hell because they cannot accept Jesus as their personal Savior.

1 John 1:8, 10 (NIV)

⁸ If we claim to be without sin, we deceive ourselves and the truth is not in us. ¹⁰ …If we claim we have not sinned, we make him out to be a liar and his word is not in us.

If we say we have no sin, we deceive ourselves, and make God a liar, His truth, His Word is not in us. We have just been told in the Bible that if we say we did not ever sin, then God's Word is not in us and that we are calling God a liar.

Romans 3:23 (NIV)

²³ For all [everyone] has sinned and fall short of the glory of God [God's standards].

Romans 6:23 (NIV)

²³ For the wages of sin is death, but the [free] gift of God is eternal life in [through] Christ Jesus our Lord.

What does God's Word say? All have sinned, not some, but all. This means every single person has sinned no matter who they are; all have sinned, except Jesus. "For the wages of sin is death." Not just some sins but sin itself, for the wages of sin is death. What did Jesus save us from? He saved us from a spiritual death. When you committed a sin, did you die? No, not physically. But the wages of sin is death. Not a physical one, but a spiritual one. When our bodies die, our spirits continue to live either in hell or in heaven. To not receive Jesus is death in hell, a death where you feel unbearable pain forever. To receive Jesus is life. To go to heaven and never feel pain again, to have eternal life with Christ forever. Remember, in John 3:7, Jesus said, "You must be born again." How much more plain does it have to be? If you have not already received Jesus Christ as your personal Savior, what are you waiting for? Receive Jesus now. God tells us how, in the following verses,

Romans 10:9–10 (ESV)

⁹ Because, if you confess with your mouth that Jesus is Lord and believe in your heart that God raised him from the dead, you will be saved.

¹⁰ For with the heart one believes and is justified, and with the mouth one confesses and is saved.

What does Romans 10:9–10 say? "*If*"—"If you confess with your mouth" (What?) "If you confess with your mouth that Jesus is Lord and believe in your heart that God raised Him from the dead, you will be saved." It did not say if you are baptized or were baptized that you would be saved. It is by confessing with your mouth that you are saved. Salvation is a gift to us. There are two things that you can do with a gift. You can reject it or receive it. If you want God's gift, you have to receive it. God made it simple for us, and the keyword is "if." If you confess with your mouth, you will be saved; if you do not confess with your mouth, you will not be saved.

"Saved from what?" The penalty for sin is an eternal spiritual death in hell. Jesus saved you from hell, the lake of fire. If you still have not prayed for salvation and you want to now, then pray the following prayer. It works. Confess with your mouth now if you have never prayed a prayer like the following prayer. If you mean it in your heart, you will go to heaven. Many have prayed this prayer or one just like it, and so have I. The prayer itself is not what saves you, but rather, it is your confession and commitment to God through Jesus Christ.

This prayer fulfills what we are told to do in Romans 10:9–10, which we have read earlier. Jesus Himself is what saves you. "Wait a minute, Mike, why say this prayer if it does not save me?" That is a good question. There are several reasons why one should say a prayer like this:

It is to fulfill Romans 10:9–10 (KJV),

> [9] That if thou shalt confess with thy mouth the Lord Jesus, and shalt believe in thine heart that God hath raised him from the dead, thou shalt be saved.
>
> [10] For with the heart man believeth unto righteousness; and with the mouth confession is made unto salvation.

It marks the moment in time when you received Jesus Christ, the gift of God. John 3:16 (KJV), "16 For God so loved the world, that he gave his only begotten Son, that whosoever believeth in him should not perish, but have everlasting life." And Ephesians 2:8 (KJV), "8 For by grace are ye saved through faith; and that not of yourselves; it is the gift of God."

It marks the moment in which you decide to become born again and ask God to forgive all your sins.

It marks the moment of your spiritual birth in Jesus Christ.

It marks the moment when you choose eternal life with Christ over eternal death.

It is to help you know and realize that you have decided to become born again.

Pray this prayer:

Dear God, I believe with all my heart that Jesus died for me. That You, God, have raised Him from the dead, and that Jesus is Lord. I repent of my sins and ask You, Jesus, for forgiveness of all my sins. I accept Your forgiveness and ask You, Jesus, to come into my heart. I accept You as my personal Savior. I commit and give my life to You. Please fill me now with the Holy Spirit. I thank You, Jesus, for saving me. In Jesus' name, I pray. Amen.

Now, if you prayed this prayer sincerely, then hallelujah! Praise the Lord! Glory to God! Praise God! Praise God! Praise

God! You are going to heaven! Hallelujah! Today is your spiritual birthday; write it down! Today, you are born again! Because *you* took the first step and accepted Jesus Christ as your personal Savior, you are born again! Yes! Glory, glory, *glory* to God! Hallelujah, glory to God! All of your sins have been forgiven, and you are going to heaven when your body dies! Yes! Your spirit is now alive because *you* received Jesus as your personal Savior! Amen! And amen!

Note: I said *you* took the first step and accepted Jesus Christ. Some Christians get technical and say there are no steps to or in being born again. I know the Bible does not say there are steps in being born again, but how else would you say it?

When you asked for forgiveness of your sins in that prayer, God forgave you of every single sin that you have ever committed. You are now fully forgiven. Here is what God said in Isaiah, Jeremiah, and Micah.

Isaiah 43:25 (NIV)

"[25] I, even I, am he who blots out your transgressions, for my own sake, and remembers your sins no more."

Jeremiah 31:34 (NIV)

[34] "No longer will they teach their neighbor, or say to one another, 'Know the LORD,' because they will all know me, from the least of them to the greatest," declares the Lord. "For I will forgive their wickedness and will remember their sins no more."

Micah 7:19 (NIV)

¹⁹ You will again have compassion on us; you will tread our sins underfoot and hurl all our iniquities into the depths of the sea.

All three of these verses talk about what God will do with our iniquities and sins after we accept Jesus as our Savior. In the first two verses, God said that He would forgive us and that He would not even remember our iniquities and sins. In Micah 7:19, God will cast the sins that we committed before we got saved into the depths of the sea.

God is saying that not only are we forgiven, but that He chose to completely forget all of our iniquities and sins when we got saved. I do not know how God can forget our sins, but that is what God is saying in these three verses. Thank You, God.

Because of those three verses, you will hear some Christians say that God threw our sins into the sea of forgetfulness. Mainly because the scripture states that He throws all our sins into the depths of the sea, and He forgets what our sins were. In Isaiah 43:25, God said that He will not remember your sins. When one does not remember, this means they forgot. Therefore, at the moment of salvation, God forgets all the sins that we have committed.

When you prayed that prayer, not only did you get forgiven of all your sins, but now the Holy Spirit has come to dwell in you. You will read about this in chapter nine. The Holy Spirit will help you to better understand the scriptures in the Bible. If you are not already in one, find and go to a Bible-believing church. As you can see, your baptism did not and does not save you. Being born again and being water-baptized are two different things.

In conclusion, even though our bodies are alive while we are sinning, our spirit is dead because sin is death. Becoming born again is a spiritual experience in which our spirit becomes alive by accepting Jesus Christ as our personal Lord and Savior. Water baptism is an outward testimony of our identification with the death and resurrection of Jesus Christ. Symbolizing our sinful self-dying and our spirit becoming alive in Christ.

Later on, I will show you scripturally that babies and little children are saved without water baptism and without receiving Jesus as their Savior. God knows our concerns for them to go to heaven, so do not worry. God has taken care of this.

Yes, I am being technical here because the words make a difference. There are those who will say that the words "born again" were supposed to be "born from above." They want to change the wording of things by their technical thinking. They do not think it through of why it says born again and not born from above. When you are born again, you are born from above because you are born of the Holy Spirit. The Holy Spirit is from above, but you are still born again because it is your second birth. First, you are born physically from your parents, and then you are born spiritually by the Holy Spirit through Jesus Christ. Your second birth is being born again. The term "born again" is correct because you are first born physically, and then you are born spiritually. Two births. The second one is your spirit was dead, and now it is alive; this is being "born again."

For those who still believe their water baptism saved them, you need to ask yourself these questions. Is water baptism alive that it can do something to save me? No. Did it die on the cross for me? No. What did water baptism do to save me? Nothing. So! How can water baptism save me when it did not do anything and cannot do anything to save me? The answer is that it can't.

Is Jesus alive, and did He do something to save me? Yes. Did He die on the cross for me? Yes. In John 3:17, did Jesus say that God sent water baptism into the world so that through it, the world might be saved? No. Did Jesus say that God sent His Son into the world so that through Him, the world might be saved? Yes. Might be saved, why? We read them earlier. Because in John 1:12, "But as many as received Him;" we must receive Him. And in Romans 10:9–10, "If we confess with our mouth believing in Jesus to be saved;" we have to confess with our mouth, Jesus, then we will be saved. Nothing being said about believing in water baptism or that it saves us.

We will get to 1 Peter 3:21 (KJV) with the phrase, "21 Even baptism doth also now save us," early in the next chapter. We will look at what Peter said before and after that phrase. You will be able to read and study the scriptures that show this phrase does not mean we are saved by our water baptism.

I am repeating this prayer to make it easy to find in this book. It is here at the end of chapter 6.

Dear God, I believe with all my heart that Jesus died for me. That You, God, have raised Him from the dead, and that Jesus is Lord. I repent of my sins and ask You, Jesus, for forgiveness of all my sins. I accept Your forgiveness and ask You, Jesus, to come into my heart. I accept You as my personal Savior. I commit and give my life to You. Please fill me now with the Holy Spirit. I thank You, Jesus, for saving me. In Jesus' name, I pray. Amen.

CHAPTER 7:

WHAT WATER BAPTISM REALLY IS

Let's look at what the Bible truly says about water baptism. Now that you are saved, you need to be baptized. We need to look at how the verses are worded. We also need to look at what the whole verse is saying and not just part of the verse so we do not take the verses out of context.

Mark 16:16 (NIV)

[16] Whoever believes and is baptized will be saved, but whoever does not believe will be condemned.

As Jesus was speaking, He put these two things in order of sequence. First, you believe, then you are baptized. Notice that in the second part of His sentence, He did not mention baptism at all. If our baptism saved us, why didn't Jesus say, "But he that believeth not and is not baptized shall be condemned." Or say, "But he that is not baptized shall be condemned." He did not say that; He said, "But he that believeth not shall be condemned" (KJV). I like how the Amplified Bible completes the meaning of what Jesus is saying, "But he who does not believe [who does not adhere to and trust in and rely on the Gospel and Him Whom it sets forth] will be condemned." According to the way that Jesus said His sentence, a person who does not believe will be condemned or not saved. A person has to believe in Jesus for themselves in order to be saved.

"Can you believe in Jesus for someone else and make them saved because you are believing for them?" The answer to your question is no because the person themself has to believe in Jesus. If our baptism saved us, then Jesus suffered and died on the cross for nothing; it was all in vain. If our baptism saved us, then Jesus would have said, "Forget this. If they can be saved by their baptism, then there is no way that I am going to die on the cross. All I have to do is to tell people that they can get saved by being baptized. Father, I am not getting whipped and dying on the cross; let their baptism save them." If we are saved by our baptism, then Jesus would have said, "He that is baptized not shall be condemned," but He didn't. He only mentioned that he who believes not shall be condemned.

If our baptism saved us, that would mean verses like John 3:16-17, "God gave us His Son to save us;" Ephesians 2:8-9, "We are saved by grace, not of works;" and Romans 10:9-10, "If we confess with our mouth and believe in our heart we will be saved," would have to be wrong, and they are not wrong. Remember, I am pointing out what God said in the Bible. God does not lie, nor does He have contradictions in the Bible.

Acts 2:38 (NIV)

[38] Peter replied, "Repent and be baptized, every one of you, in the name of Jesus Christ for the forgiveness of your sins. And you will receive the gift of the Holy Spirit."

We have just read in the Bible, repent and be baptized. It does not say or support the one phrase in the Bible, "Even baptism doth also now save us." "What? But Mike, the verse does say, 'Even baptism doth also now save us.'" I know. We will get to that in a little bit. Please be patient with me; we will get to that verse, and when we get there, you will see that is not the whole verse. To get the full meaning of what this phrase means, "Even baptism doth also now save us," we need to read the whole verse and not just part of it and look at how the whole verse is worded. First, I need to show you some things before I get to that verse. Now, let's read on.

Jesus was an adult when He got baptized. He set the example for us.

Matthew 3:13–17 (NIV)

[13] Then Jesus came from Galilee to the Jordan to be baptized by John.

[14] But John tried to deter him, saying, "I need to be baptized by you, and do you come to me?"

[15] Jesus replied, "Let it be so now; it is proper for us to do this to fulfill all righteousness." Then John consented.

[16] As soon as Jesus was baptized, he went up out of the water. At that moment heaven was opened, and he saw the Spirit of God descending like a dove and alighting on him.

[17] And a voice from heaven said, "This is my Son, whom I love; with him I am well pleased."

This was the only time that Jesus got baptized in His life. Jesus was carrying out what God requires of Him and us. He was setting the example for us. John was baptizing believers. As we read, when Jesus came up out of the water, the Holy Spirit came upon Jesus, and God said that He was well pleased with Him. Note: John was not baptizing babies. Not once does God teach in the Bible to baptize babies.

Now, let's go to the book of Acts to view baptism after Jesus' death and resurrection.

Acts 2:38–41 (NIV)

[38] Peter replied, "Repent and be baptized, every one of you, in the name of Jesus Christ for the forgiveness of your sins. And you will receive the gift of the Holy Spirit.

[39] The promise is for you and your children and for all who are far off—for all whom the Lord our God will call."

[40] With many other words he warned them; and he pleaded with them, "Save yourselves from this corrupt generation."

[41] Those who accepted his message were baptized, and about three thousand were added to their number that day.

If you open your Bible and read Acts chapter 2, verses 14 through 37, you will see that Peter preached a message to a crowd of people. After the people heard Peter's message in verse 37, they asked a question. The last four words in verse 37 are the question, "What shall we do?" Starting with verse 38, we read the answer. Peter said to them, "Repent and be baptized for the forgiveness of your sins." In verse 40, by how it is worded, "With many other words he warned them," Peter must have preached another message. Peter most likely preached a message on salvation because of what happened next in verse 41. "Those who accepted his message were baptized." They heard, accepted, and were baptized.

My point is, first, they heard the message, then they received the message, which most likely was the message of salvation (accepting Jesus Christ as your Savior), and then they were baptized. It is the order God has set for us. They did not get baptized until after they heard and received the message. The people were saved first, and then they were baptized. "Mike, If water baptism does not save us, then why get baptized?" First of all, because we are commanded to be baptized, as you have read in the Bible, "Repent and be baptized every one of you." These were adults being baptized, not babies. They were baptized because they believed and received Jesus. Let us dig and see what water baptism is.

1 Peter 3:18–21

(KJV), "[18] For Christ also hath once suffered for sins, the just for the unjust, that he might bring us to God, being put to death in the flesh, but quickened by the Spirit:

[19] By which also he went and preached unto the spirits in prison;

[20] Which sometime were disobedient, when once the longsuffering of God waited in the days of Noah, while the ark was a preparing, wherein few, that is, eight souls were saved by water.

[21] The like figure whereunto even baptism doth also now save us (not the putting away of the filth of the flesh, but the answer of a good conscience toward God,) by the resurrection of Jesus Christ."

(AMP), "[18] For Christ [the Messiah Himself] died for sins once for all, the Righteous for the unrighteous (the Just for the unjust, the Innocent for the guilty), that He might bring us to God. In His human body He was put to death, but He was made alive in the spirit,

[19] In which He went and preached to the spirits in prison,

[20] [The souls of those] who long before in the days of Noah had been disobedient, when God's patience waited during the building of the ark in which a few [people], actually eight in number; were saved through water.

[21] And baptism, which is a figure [of their deliverance], does now also save you [from inward questionings and fears], not by the removing of outward body filth [bathing], but by [providing you with] the answer of a good and clear conscience (inward cleanness and peace) before God [because you are demonstrating what you believe to be yours] through the resurrection of Jesus Christ."

(NLT), "¹⁸ Christ suffered for our sins once for all time. He never sinned, but he died for sinners to bring you safely home to God. He suffered physical death, but he was raised to life in the Spirit.

¹⁹ So he went and preached to the spirits in prison—

²⁰ those who disobeyed God long ago when God waited patiently while Noah was building his boat. Only eight people were saved from drowning in that terrible flood.

²¹ And that water is a picture of baptism, which now saves you, not by removing dirt from your body, but as a response to God from a clear conscience. It is effective because of the resurrection of Jesus Christ."

(NIV), "¹⁸ For Christ also suffered once for sins, the righteous for the unrighteous, to bring you to God. He was put to death in the body but made alive in the Spirit.

¹⁹ After being made alive, he went and made proclamation to the imprisoned spirits—

²⁰ to those who were disobedient long ago when God waited patiently in the days of Noah while the ark was being built. In it only a few people, eight in all, were saved through water,

²¹ and this water symbolizes baptism that now saves you also—not the removal of dirt from the body but the pledge of a clear conscience toward God. It saves you by the resurrection of Jesus Christ."

In verse 18, we read Christ died once for all time. This means that no more sacrifices have to be made for our sins. Jesus Christ, "the righteous one for the unrighteous," which is the world (us). Jesus died to bring you to God. In verses 19 and 20, Jesus Christ "preached to the spirits that were in prison." The prison these spirits were in is hell, of course, unless you know of a human prison that holds spirits as prisoners. They are the spirits of the people who disobeyed God when Noah was building the ark. Only eight people were saved through the water. Think about it. The water did not save the eight people; the ark did because the water drowned everyone else.

Verse 21 (KJV), "The like figure whereunto even baptism."

(AMP), "And baptism, which is a figure [of their deliverance]."

(NLT), "And that water is a picture of baptism."

And in the (NIV), it says, "And this water symbolizes baptism."

This part of verse 21 in each version is saying that baptism is "a figure of Noah's flood, being the same as;" "a figure of their deliverance;" "that the water is a picture of baptism;" "this water symbolizes baptism." In other words, water baptism is like the flood water after Noah built the ark. The phrase that follows, "Even baptism which now saves us," strongly indicates and says that water baptism is a figure and representation of salvation. Peter is comparing water baptism to the flood water of Noah and, in a sense, saying they are alike. The flood waters killed all the disobedient people. God had eight people that were obedient to Him in the ark. If Noah had not built the ark, then no one would have survived the flood.

Verse 20 says that the eight were saved by water, but being in the ark is what saved Noah and the seven other people. Going under the water (the people), the sinful man (men) died. The ark rising up by the water from the ground saved the righteous man (men) to live a new life. The water is not what saved them; the ark is what saved them. When the flood water was gone, they were to live a new life which was to be without sin. The ark is symbolic of Jesus Christ in our salvation.

The ark was tossed around by the water. The ark kept Noah and the seven from drowning. The ark saved the eight, not the water. Jesus Christ is what saved us, not our water baptism. What did the flood water do? The flood water drowned and killed all the sinful people. It did not save anyone. Just like Noah's flood water did not save anyone, water baptism does not save anyone. The flood water of Noah's day drowned all the sinners; water baptism is symbolically the same in that going under the water represents our dying to our sinful man (drowning the sinful man) to live a life without sin.

At the beginning of verse 21, God has Peter comparing water baptism to the flood water of Noah's time, saying they are the same. Why do we want to use something to say it saves us when it is compared to something that killed all but eight people in the world? If they are the same, which they are, what is the water baptism killing? We will soon find out the answer.

Let us look very carefully at the second part of verse 21 of 1 Peter chapter 3. As I explain this verse, I want you to keep in mind how the verse is worded in each translation. They are worded differently but have the same meaning. Please stay with me on this.

"Baptism, which now saves you;" looking at this part of the verse, one would say, "Ha, ha. See? You are saved by your baptism!" But, because of how the rest of verse 21 is worded,

I will show you that is not what Peter meant. Then Peter said, "Not by removing dirt from your body." This gives an indication of baptism washing something, not saving someone. In the latter part of verse 21, Peter is saying water baptism does not remove dirt from our bodies but shows what now saves us.

Water baptism shows that we no longer have a bad conscience, not by washing dirt off of the flesh but by washing off the guilt of our conscience. Our conscience was washed and made clean from all the guilt of our sins. We are able to have a good conscience toward God because when we receive Jesus and ask for the forgiveness of our sins, our conscience becomes free from the guilt of sin.

The words that follow next are "but the answer." But, like the word if, is a small word with a big meaning. "Baptism which now also saves you but,"—but!—"But the answer." That "but" is there for a reason. When the word "but" is put with the words "the answer" in the English language, it means: here is the real answer. The real answer is that you are not saved by your water baptism, "but the [real] answer [is] of a good [clean] conscience toward God and by the resurrection of Jesus Christ." Thank God for that little word "but." Baptism is an outward manifestation (an outward testimony) of our inward conversion.

Yes, in verse 21, Peter said, "Water baptism which now saves you." Then, Peter said what really saves you by saying the three keywords in that verse. They are "but the answer." But the answer is we have a good, clean, guiltless conscience toward God and have been saved by the resurrection of Jesus Christ, now we can get baptized. Who saved us? Jesus Christ. God gave us His Son (not water baptism) so that we might be saved.

In verse 21, Peter is saying that your baptism is showing what saved you. You were not saved with water baptism by washing dirt off of the flesh, but by the washing of your sins and guilt from your conscience toward God, by the resurrection of Jesus Christ. The ark is symbolic of Jesus. The ark saved the eight people; Jesus saved you.

Open your Bible to Romans 10:9–10. Can a baby do what these verses are saying before it is baptized? Does a baby know what the resurrection of Jesus Christ is all about before it is baptized? No, therefore, a baby is not saved through water baptism. Later, I will explain scripturally why babies without water baptism will still go to heaven if/or when they die.

Yes, I am repeating myself, but because of the wording of the verses, I feel this will make it very clear what Peter really meant. Peter is comparing water baptism to the flood water of Noah's day. The verse said that water baptism is like Noah's flood water. The flood water did not save the eight people; the ark did. The waters of baptism are not what saves us; we are saved by the death and resurrection of Jesus Christ, by the shedding of His blood for the forgiveness of our sins. At the beginning of verse 21, we are told that water baptism is like a figure of and/or a picture of Noah's flood water, showing us the symbolic part of the old man in us dying to our sinful ways. Reading verse 21, taking the whole verse, it is saying that water baptism is a representation of our salvation. The answer is that we are saved by our good conscience toward God, saved by the resurrection of Jesus Christ. Water baptism confirms that we have decided to die to our sinful life and to live a new life in Christ Jesus.

Romans 6:1–7 (ESV)

¹What shall we say then? Are we to continue in sin that grace may abound?

²By no means! How can we who died to sin still live in it?

³Do you not know that all of us who have been baptized into Christ Jesus were baptized into his death?

⁴We were buried therefore with him by baptism into death, in order that, just as Christ was raised from the dead by the glory of the Father, we too might walk in newness of life.

⁵For if we have been united with him in a death like his, we shall certainly be united with him in a resurrection like his.

⁶We know that our old self was crucified with him in order that the body of sin might be brought to nothing, so that we would no longer be enslaved to sin.

⁷For one who has died has been set free from sin.

Notice in verse four we were buried with him by baptism into death. Baptism into death, not into salvation. Being baptized into death is not being saved.

As we read these seven verses along with 1 Peter 3:21 we see that we are demonstrating what has happened to us spiritually when we got saved. In baptism (spiritually speaking), when we go under the water, we show that the old sinful man in us has died (drowned) and that we are spiritually crucified and buried with Christ. When we come up out of the water, we have risen with Christ to a new life in Jesus Christ. In a literal sense, we are washing the old sinful man off our spirit. When we come up out of the water, it signifies that our sins have been washed away. With our water baptism, our spirit is now completely cleansed of our sins and is now alive in and with Jesus Christ. So! In water baptism, we are buried with Christ, and we are raised with Him to a new life.

Acts 22:16 (ESV)

[16] And now why do you wait? Rise and be baptized and wash away your sins, calling on his name.

Water baptism does not wash away the filth of the flesh but symbolizes our sins being washed away by the blood of Jesus Christ, a representation of our spirit being brought to life from the dead. What saved us is our good conscience toward God and the resurrection of Jesus Christ (1 Peter 3:21). This happens by doing what it says in Romans 10:9–10.

Now, if our water baptism saved us, why didn't Jesus go around saying get baptized so you can be saved? But Jesus said in John 3:16, "God so loved the world that He gave us His Son that you might be saved." If water baptism really would save us, Jesus would have told us to baptize our babies so that they would be saved. Even though God the Father and God the Son (Jesus) want everyone to get saved, not once did Jesus ever say to baptize babies to save them or that by your water baptism, you are saved. Never did Jesus say that being born again is the same as water baptism.

God's Word does not say water baptism is what makes you born again.

If your water baptism could save you, then that is what Jesus would have preached. If being saved by our water baptism is true, then Jesus did not have to come to Earth and die on the cross. If our water baptism saves us, then why does it say in Romans 10:9–10, "If you confess with your mouth, you shall be saved"? It does not say, "If you get or got baptized, you shall be saved," or "If you confess with your mouth, your baptism will save you," but it says, "If you confess with your mouth that Jesus is Lord, you shall be saved." What Romans 10:9–10 implies is if you do not confess with your mouth to God, then you are not saved. If our baptism saved us, then Romans 10:9–10 would be a contradiction in the Bible, and there are no contradictions in the Bible.

Before Jesus went to heaven, He said this,

Matthew 28:18–20 (NIV)

[18] All authority in heaven and on earth has been given to me.

[19] Therefore go and make disciples of all nations, baptizing them in the name of the Father and of the Son and of the Holy Spirit,

[20] and teaching them to obey everything I have commanded you. And surely I am with you always, to the very end of the age.

Mark 16:15–16 (NIV)

"[15] Go into all the world and preach the gospel to all creation. [16] Whoever believes and is baptized will be saved, but whoever does not believe will be condemned."

Jesus has said, "Go preach the gospel to all nations." Then He said, "Baptizing them in the name of the Father and of the Son and of the Holy Spirit." First, preach the gospel, then baptize them. Jesus said, "He who believes and is baptized shall be saved." Then, Jesus made a distinction between salvation and baptism. He said, "But whoever does not believe will be condemned." In this part of His statement, He left out baptism. Jesus said nothing about baptism in the second part of His sentence, "But if you do not believe, you will be condemned." Nothing is said if you are not baptized that you will be condemned.

In reading the Bible, you will notice that words like receive, believe, heard, and repent always come first before the word baptized. It will say, those who have received and are baptized, or those who have believed and are baptized, or those who heard and were baptized, or repent and be baptized, and you will be saved. The word baptized is second because you have to hear, believe, receive, and repent to be saved before you are baptized. Therefore, your baptism does not save you. But you still need to be baptized because Jesus commanded it. Let's move on.

You will be saved if you confess with your mouth the Lord Jesus Christ, accepting and receiving God's gift, Jesus Christ. There is nothing said about water baptism saving you. To say that your water baptism saved you is a contradiction to Romans 10:9-10. There are no contradictions in the Bible.

Now, are you going to believe what the Bible says about water baptism or still believe what your religion says about water baptism? Who is correct, God or religion? Who is man to say that God is wrong? Take the verses we read and study them again.

Remember, when taking just part of a verse or verses, a person can make it say whatever they want it to say, but as a whole, a person cannot. There is an old saying that is not in the Bible, but it seems to be true. *The truth hurts.* I did not intend to offend anyone, but God and I wanted you to know what God says in the Bible about what to believe regarding water baptism.

At the beginning of this chapter, I said Jesus was an adult when He was baptized. When He was eight days old, He was circumcised and presented to the Lord God the Father. I do not want to teach or get into the spiritual ritual of circumcision that Jews practiced in the Old Testament. But I will say this much on it. I was told circumcision is a rite of passage. It identifies the person as belonging to their tribe—in this case, belonging to God. Jews still practice this today. It's a special occasion called a Bris. This is not a form of salvation as to the baby going to heaven if the baby were to die. In Luke 2:21, Jesus was circumcised. In verse 22, Mary was purified, and Jesus was presented to the Lord.

Mary, like any other woman after giving birth, was considered unclean and had to be purified, and she was purified according to the law of Moses. You can read about the purification in Luke 2:21–40 and Leviticus chapter 12. You can learn about biblical circumcision by reading and studying the Bible. Remember, Jesus was an adult when He was water-baptized.

Jesus is our example in life. Today, most Bible-believing churches have baby dedication services. Parents publicly dedicate and present their baby to the Lord and promise to raise their child up in the Lord. The congregation agrees to be supportive of the parents in raising their child in the Lord.

Ephesians 6:4 (KJV)

"⁴And, ye fathers, provoke not your children to wrath: but bring them up in the nurture and admonition of the Lord."

We are commanded to bring them up in the nurture and admonition of the Lord. We make the promise of obeying and doing His command to bring them up to know and love the Lord. Then, we stand on His promise.

Proverbs 22:6 (KJV)

⁶Train up a child in the way he should go: and when he is old, he will not depart from it.

Baby dedication is not a replacement for water baptism, and it does not save the child. Not once do you read of a baby being baptized in the Bible; it is always adults. Baby dedication is a time of celebration in presenting our babies to God. Committing ourselves to training our children in the ways of the Lord.

In the next chapter, I will show you scripturally that babies and little children are saved even though they did not receive Jesus as their Savior and without water baptism. God knows our concerns for them to go to heaven if they die, so do not worry. God has taken care of this.

CHAPTER 8:

WHERE DO BABIES AND LITTLE CHILDREN GO WHEN THEY DIE?

"Because our baptism does not save us, what happens to babies and little children? Do they go to hell or heaven? Why should we become as little children to enter God's kingdom?" Those are good questions. Before I answer your questions, I want to say one thing. Our God is a merciful God.

Deuteronomy 1:30–39 (NIV)

[30] The LORD our God, who is going before you, will fight for you, as he did for you in Egypt, before your very eyes,

[31] and in the wilderness. There you saw how the LORD your God carried you, as a father carries his son, all the way you went until you reached this place.

[32] In spite of this, you did not trust in the LORD your God,

[33] who went ahead of you on your journey, in fire by night and in a cloud by day, to search out places for you to camp and to show you the way you should go.

[34] When the LORD heard what you said, he was angry and solemnly swore:

⁳⁵ "No one from this evil generation shall see the good land I swore to give your ancestors,

³⁶ except Caleb son of Jephunneh. He will see it, and I will give him and his descendants the land he set his feet on, because he followed the LORD wholeheartedly."

³⁷ Because of you the LORD became angry with me also and said, "You shall not enter it, either.

³⁸ But your assistant, Joshua son of Nun, will enter it. Encourage him, because he will lead Israel to inherit it.

³⁹ And the little ones that you said would be taken captive, your children who do not yet know good from bad—they will enter the land. I will give it to them and they will take possession of it."

You will have to wait until we get to verse 39 to see God's mercy. In reading the books of Moses, you will notice even while Moses was leading his people out of Egypt they were still disobedient to God at one time or another. As you can see in the verses that we just read, God was upset with their continued disobedience toward Him. God was so upset with all who were disobedient that He did not let them go into the land of Canaan as He had promised them. Only the obedient ones could go in, like Joshua and Caleb.

Now, to the good part. Let us read verse 39 again. This is God's mercy.

Deuteronomy 1:39 (NIV)

³⁹ "And the little ones that you said would be taken captive, your children who do not yet know good from bad—they will enter the land. I will give it to them and they will take possession of it."

Verse 39 talks about the little children who belong to those who will not live to go into Canaan and possess the land. The little children will not be punished for the sins of their parents' disobedience to God. Those little ones who have "no knowledge between good and evil" (KJV), "cannot discern between good and evil" (AMP), and "who did not yet know good from bad" (NIV) were saved. They were too young to learn, know, or understand good and evil. God said the little children would not be preyed on or be taken captive. They were saved and went with the obedient ones into the land of Canaan to possess the land. God had mercy on the little children and saved them because of their innocence.

Matthew 18:1-4 (NIV),

¹ At that time the disciples came to Jesus and asked, "Who, then, is the greatest in the kingdom of heaven?"

² He called a little child to him, and placed the child among them.

³ And he said: "Truly I tell you, unless you change and become like little children, you will never enter the kingdom of heaven.

⁴ Therefore, whoever takes the lowly position of this child is the greatest in the kingdom of heaven.

Matthew 19:13–14 (NIV),

¹³ Then people brought little children to Jesus for him to place his hands on them and pray for them. But the disciples rebuked them.

¹⁴ Jesus said, "Let the little children come to me, and do not hinder them, for the kingdom of heaven belongs to such as these."

Mark 10:14 and Luke 18:16 say the same as in Matthew 19:14: that the kingdom of heaven belongs to the little children.

What are some of the things that little children do with their parents? They trust in, rely on, believe in, and remain steadfast to their parents. A baby totally trusts in and relies on his/her parents, or in these days, parent. The disciples asked, "Who is the greatest in the kingdom of heaven?" Jesus answered by saying, "Whoever humbles himself like a little child is the greatest in the kingdom of heaven."

What Jesus is saying in verse 4 is that we have to become like little children in order to be great in heaven. In verse 14 (KJV), Jesus said, "For of such is the kingdom of heaven." "For the kingdom of heaven belongs to such as these [the little children]" (NIV). Jesus is saying heaven is theirs; they are saved. Jesus is saying in verse 3 that we are to change, be converted, repent (be born again), and become like the little children in order to be great in the kingdom of heaven.

We are to humble ourselves and become as little children, for the kingdom of heaven belongs to the little children. We are to totally trust in and rely on, believe in, and remain steadfast with God, and to repent, to not be guilty of sin, in order to enter and be great in the kingdom of heaven. This is a part of our salvation, of being born again.

Why does the kingdom of heaven belong to little children? Because of their innocence, they have no knowledge of good and evil, cannot discern between good and evil, and do not yet know good from bad. They have no knowledge of what sin is.

Just as we were until the age of accountability, babies and little children are going to heaven. With all of what these verses say, how can anyone say that little children and babies are not going to heaven because they are not baptized? Remember, water baptism does not save you. If we are not saved by water baptism, then little children and babies are not saved by water baptism either.

All the verses in this chapter talk about little children. The little children that are being talked about are those who have "no knowledge between good and evil," "cannot discern between good and evil," and "who do not yet know [understand] good from bad." These verses show God's mercy in that little children and babies are saved and going to heaven because of their innocence in not knowing right from wrong or what sin is. But once they grow out of that innocence, once they learn and understand good and evil, right and wrong, that is when they have to receive Jesus Christ as their personal Savior in order to be saved.

Just because a child knows that he or she cannot do certain things because they are told by their parents they are wrong or bad does not mean the child understands why he or she cannot do them. It does not mean they know what sin is.

When a child starts to really understand right from wrong, what sin really is, is when it is time [on their level] to teach them about salvation in Jesus Christ. Therefore, little children and babies are not to be baptized to get saved because they are already saved until the age of accountability. For as we have read earlier our baptism does not save us. God knew that we would all be concerned about our babies and little ones. God has shown us in these verses that He has made this one exception for little children because of their innocence; this includes toddlers and infants. If they die, they are going to heaven without being baptized, "for of such is the kingdom of heaven."

It is neither biblical nor scriptural to baptize babies. God did not tell us to baptize babies; man did; it is a man-made belief. Baptizing babies is a contradiction to God's Word. As we learned in the beginning of chapter 7, Jesus was an adult when He got baptized.

Note: See Luke 2:22 and Mark 10:16 in the Bible. His parents dedicated Him to God when He was a baby.

We are to humble ourselves and become as little children because they trust in, rely on, believe in, and remain steadfast to their parents and are not held guilty of sin. To become as little children, we have to trust in, rely on, believe in, and remain steadfast to God.

Water baptism does not save anyone, including babies. Babies are saved until they get to the point in their lives where they understand and discern right from wrong and know what sin is. Once they reach that point in life, they are no longer saved and need to be born again by accepting Jesus as their Savior.

CHAPTER 9:

THE HOLY SPIRIT DWELLING IN YOU

There is a lot to say about the Holy Spirit dwelling in you. But God just wants me to show that when you receive Jesus Christ as your personal Savior, the Holy Spirit comes and dwells in your body with you.

"Mike, do you mean that the Holy Spirit is dwelling in all of those who are born again?" Good question. The answer is yes. The Holy Spirit dwells in all born-again believers. Let's look at the following verses.

Titus 3:3–7 (ESV)

³ For we ourselves were once foolish, disobedient, led astray, slaves to various passions and pleasures, passing our days in malice and envy, hated by others and hating one another.

⁴ But when the goodness and loving kindness of God our Savior appeared,

⁵ he saved us, not because of works done by us in righteousness, but according to his own mercy, by the washing of regeneration and renewal of the Holy Spirit,

⁶ whom he poured out on us richly through Jesus Christ our Savior,

⁷ so that being justified by his grace we might become heirs according to the hope of eternal life.

As we can see in Titus 3:3-7, we were living a life of sin, but through Jesus Christ, our sins were washed away, and we were given a new birth and a new life. Now, being born again, we have been given eternal life to live with God forever. Yes, we are not perfect, but with the help of the Holy Spirit, we will be able to live our lives to the best of our abilities without sin. This is why the Holy Spirit comes and dwells in us: to help us live a life without sin and to help us understand the Bible.

Romans 8:15-16 (ESV)

¹⁵ For you did not receive the spirit of slavery to fall back into fear, but you have received the Spirit of adoption as sons, by whom we cry, "Abba! Father!"

¹⁶ The Spirit himself bears witness with our spirit that we are children of God.

Now that you have received Jesus as your personal Savior, the Holy Spirit has come to live with you and in you. The Holy Spirit now dwells in you. You have become a child of God.

You did not receive a spirit of fear as to being a slave to God. But you received God's Spirit; you received the Holy Spirit. God's Spirit is in your body with your spirit. So, not only did Jesus take your punishment for your sins and save you from hell, but Jesus made you a part of His family when you accepted Him as your personal Savior. Everyone who is truly born again is your brother or sister in Jesus Christ.

Jesus said in John 14:15–23 (ESV),

¹⁵ "If you love me, you will keep my commandments.

¹⁶ And I will ask the Father, and he will give you another Helper, to be with you forever,

¹⁷ even the Spirit of truth, whom the world cannot receive, because it neither sees him nor knows him. You know him, for he dwells with you and will be in you.

¹⁸ I will not leave you as orphans; I will come to you.

¹⁹ Yet a little while and the world will see me no more, but you will see me. Because I live, you also will live.

²⁰ In that day you will know that I am in my Father, and you in me, and I in you.

²¹ Whoever has my commandments and keeps them, he it is who loves me. And he who loves me will be loved by my Father, and I will love him and manifest myself to him."

²² Judas (not Iscariot) said to him, "Lord, how is it that you will manifest yourself to us, and not to the world?"

²³ Jesus answered him, "If anyone loves me, he will keep my word, and my Father will love him, and we will come to him and make our home with him."

At the end of verse 17, Jesus is saying that the Holy Spirit dwells with you and will be in you. At the end of verse 20, Jesus is saying that He, Jesus, will be in you. In verses 17–20, Jesus is saying that both He and the Holy Spirit will dwell in us after He permanently returns to heaven.

Romans 8:9-11 (NIV)

⁹ You, however, are not in the realm of the flesh but are in the realm of the Spirit, if indeed the Spirit of God lives in you. And if anyone does not have the Spirit of Christ, they do not belong to Christ.

¹⁰ But if Christ is in you, then even though your body is subject to death because of sin, the Spirit gives life because of righteousness.

¹¹ And if the Spirit of him who raised Jesus from the dead is living in you, he who raised Christ from the dead will also give life to your mortal bodies because of his Spirit who lives in you.

1 John 3:24 (NIV)

"²⁴ The one who keeps God's commandments lives in him, and he in them. And this is how we know that he lives in us: We know it by the Spirit he gave us."

With the Holy Spirit in us, our sinful nature, the flesh, no longer has control over us. You have the power to say "no" to your flesh and "no" to sin in your life because you have the Holy Spirit dwelling in you. Notice that in Romans 8:9, God first had Paul write the Spirit of God and then the Spirit of Christ. There is only one Spirit that is being talked about here, and that is the Holy Spirit. God and Jesus have the same Spirit. The Holy Spirit and Jesus dwell in you. When you became born again, according to the Bible, the Holy Spirit came to dwell in you. Therefore, God, Jesus, and the Holy Spirit are always with you and dwell in you.

Talk about a mind-blower! The Holy Spirit is dwelling right now in every person on this earth who is truly born again, according to the Bible. The Holy Spirit is dwelling in millions of people all at the same time. With God, all things are possible. Another mind-blower is in Romans 8:9–11; read it again. These verses alone show the one God in three being one God. Wow!

As you read the Bible, you will find other verses that show you that the Holy Spirit now dwells in you. The Holy Spirit is with you everywhere you go now for the rest of your life. Not only does the Holy Spirit dwell in you, but Jesus Christ dwells in you, too.

The Holy Spirit could not dwell in any born-again person until after Jesus permanently went to heaven. So, those who were saved before Jesus Christ died on the cross and went to heaven did not have the Holy Spirit dwelling in them. The day of Pentecost is the beginning of when the Holy Spirit started to dwell in believers (Acts 2:4). From then on, the Holy Spirit dwells in a person from the moment they are born again.

The Holy Spirit cannot dwell in a person if they are not born again because they are not saved, and He is promised only to those who become born again. We read this in Acts chapters one and two.

CHAPTER 10:

Repenting Is a Part of Loving God

In John 14:15, Jesus said that if you love Him, then you will keep and obey His commandments. Now that you are born again, Jesus wants you to keep and obey His commandments. What Jesus is saying is that by obeying Him, you are showing Him that you love Him. Obeying Jesus is not an option. If!—is a big if—"If you love Me, keep My commandments." God and Jesus love you. Jesus is not just talking about the ten commandments. He is also talking about all the commands that are given to you in the New Testament and other commands in the Old Testament that are not a part of the ten commandments. "How will I know all of God's and Jesus' commandments or commands?" Another good question! The answer is by reading the Bible on a daily basis. Start reading the New Testament first, then the Old Testament, because the New Testament is God's new covenant with you and is the fulfillment of the Old Testament. God has given us a lot of commands throughout the New Testament. God wants you to obey all of His commands, not just some of them or only the ones that are convenient for you to obey.

Remember, Jesus said (in Matthew 7:21, chapter 6), "Not everyone that says, 'Lord, Lord' to Him will enter the kingdom of heaven but he that does the will of His Father will enter." If you try to keep the ten commandments on your own, you will fail. But if you obey God's and Jesus' commands in the Bible, with the help of the Holy Spirit, you will eventually not fail. Some sinful things you will be able to stop right away, others you will not because not everyone can change overnight. If you try to stop sinning before you get saved, it will never happen because you do not have the Holy Spirit in you. No one can stop sinning without the help of the Holy Spirit. God, through Jesus Christ and the Holy Spirit, will help you to overcome sin.

It is hard to obey God completely if you do not read the Bible. Yes, I am helping you to understand God's Word, but you still have to read the Bible so you know for sure that what I am saying is indeed what God's Word is saying.

When you read the Bible, God puts His Word in your heart. When God puts His Word in your heart it is easier to obey God.

Hebrews 8:10 (KJV)

¹⁰ For this is the covenant that I will make with the house of Israel after those days, saith the Lord; I will put my laws into their mind, and write them in their hearts: and I will be to them a God, and they shall be to me a people.

In the later part of 1 John 2:14 (KJV), "The word of God abideth in you."

Go back to chapter 9, and look at John 14:15–23 again. Notice that Jesus said, "If you love me, obey my commandments." "Those who accept my commandments and obey them are the ones who love me." Jesus said that those who obey His commandments (in other places in the Bible, it will say commands) "are the ones who love" Him. I want to point out a couple of things here. Jesus said to obey His commandments. Whenever God the Father or God the Son (Jesus) talk about obeying their commandments or commands, they are talking only about the ones in the Bible and the ones that line up with the rest of the Bible. They always say My commandments or commands. Never do you ever see it said in the Bible, "If you love Me, obey man-made commandments or commands." It is always, "If you love Me, obey My commandments or commands."

Where do you find His commands and commandments? In the Bible. God does not want us to ever obey or believe man-made commandments or commands. The Bible says to be a doer of the Word. The Bible does not say to be a doer of man-made beliefs. That is why I say if your beliefs are not found in the Bible or they do not line up with the Bible, then they are wrong. But God still wants you to obey the laws of your country. You don't have to believe in them, but you still have to obey them. Remember, God, through the Holy Spirit, told man what to write in the Bible. Man himself did not give us the Bible.

"Can a believer show God and Jesus that he or she does not love Them?" Yes. "How?" By not obeying Their commandments or commands. God and Jesus both said, "If you love Me, obey My commandments." Parents feel the same way when a child disobeys them. *And* they feel hurt. Think about it. When we are disobedient to God we are showing Him that we do not love Him. "If—If anyone loves Me, he will keep My commandments." Keeping God's commandments is how we show Him that we love Him.

Now, let us look at some of God's commands for us today. God commands us to repent; it is not an option.

Matthew 3:2 (ESV)

² "Repent, for the kingdom of heaven is at hand."

Matthew 4:17 (KJV)

¹⁷ From that time Jesus began to preach, and to say, "Repent: for the kingdom of heaven is at hand."

Mark 1:15 (KJV)

¹⁵ And saying, The time is fulfilled, and the kingdom of God is at hand: repent ye, and believe the gospel.

Mark 6:12 (KJV)

¹² And they went out, and preached that men should repent.

Acts 3:19 (KJV)

¹⁹ Repent ye therefore, and be converted, that your sins may be blotted out, when the times of refreshing shall come from the presence of the Lord.

Acts 17:30 (ESV)

³⁰ The times of ignorance God overlooked, but now he commands all people everywhere to repent.

Acts 26:20 (ESV),

²⁰ But declared first to those in Damascus, then in Jerusalem and throughout all the region of Judea, and also to the Gentiles, that they should repent and

turn to God, performing deeds in keeping with their repentance.

"What does repent mean?" Good question. Repent means to change one's mind, to turn away from the sinful things in your life. To feel remorseful for the sins you have done. To turn away is to stop sinning. We do not stop sinning overnight, but with the help of the Holy Spirit, Jesus, and God, we can stop sinning every day of our lives. The verses of God's Word tell us to repent and change our minds. This means to turn away from sin and think differently. "How do we do that?" One, by reading the Bible. When you read the Bible you renew your mind in what God wants you to believe and how God wants you to live. God puts His laws in your heart. Two, by lining your life up with the Word, following Jesus' example, and obeying His commands; this will help you to overcome sin in your life.

"Who are the Gentiles?" I am glad you asked that question. Anyone who is not born of Jewish descent is a Gentile, no matter what their beliefs are. So! If you are not a Jew, then you are a Gentile. Even after you get saved you are still a Gentile. As we can see, it is very important to God that we repent of our sins. Repentance was and still is preached to everyone, even to the Gentiles.

"So, Mike, do we ever become perfect?" In God's eyes, yes, we do. "Are you perfect, Mike?" No, because no one on Earth is perfect, but I am going to heaven because I have accepted Jesus Christ as my personal Savior, and I have put all my faith in Jesus Christ, who has saved me. I am born again. I strive to live an obedient life to God. "Mike, what happens when you do sin?" That is another good question.

God's Word says in 1 John 2:1–2 (KJV),

¹ My little children, these things write I unto you, that ye sin not. And if any man sin, we have an advocate with the Father, Jesus Christ the righteous:

² And he is the propitiation for our sins: and not for ours only, but also for the sins of the whole world.

1 John 1:9 (NLT)

⁹ But if we confess our sins to him, he is faithful and just to forgive us our sins and to cleanse us from all wickedness.

"Propitiation" means the turning away of wrath by an offering, in our case, the turning away of the wrath of God. This means satisfying the wrath of God by the atoning sacrifice of Jesus Christ for our sins.

The atoning sacrifice is the suffering, beating, shedding of blood, and death of Jesus Christ. This is the only offering that could turn away the wrath of God for us.

If we do sin, we have an advocate, Jesus Christ, and He will intercede for us, and we will be forgiven. "Does this mean that I can continue to go on sinning?" I am glad you asked that question. The answer to your question is no. We are to strive to stop sinning. "So why should I strive to stop sinning?" According to the Bible, a Christian is not supposed to continue living a life of sin. Let's look at some verses that will answer your question.

Luke 13:1-5 (ESV)

¹ There were some present at that very time who told him about the Galileans whose blood Pilate had mingled with their sacrifices.

² And he answered them, "Do you think that these Galileans were worse sinners than all the other Galileans, because they suffered in this way?

³ No, I tell you; but unless you repent, you will all likewise perish.

⁴ Or those eighteen on whom the tower in Siloam fell and killed them: do you think that they were worse offenders than all the others who lived in Jerusalem?

⁵ No, I tell you; but unless you repent, you will all likewise perish."

Let's look at the point Jesus is showing us by what He is saying here and how He is saying it. Jesus is pointing out that no matter what sin you have committed, sin is sin. If you just tell a lie, or if you commit a violent killing, sin is sin. To God, one sin is no worse than another. A violent killing is no worse than a lie. To us humans, a violent killing is much worse than a lie. Jesus is saying it does not matter what your sin is, it is a sin against God. Unless you repent of your sins (turn away from sin or stop sinning constantly), "you too, likewise, will perish." So, we must strive to live a life without sin, or we, too, will perish. "Will perish," meaning will not go to heaven. "Mike, many of the fun things I do in life are sinful. How will I have any fun in life without them?"

I, too, thought my life would be really boring without all of the sinful things that I did. There are many fun things to do in life that are not sinful. When I got saved, I was twenty-one years old, and I still wanted to have a lot of fun in my life. I did and still do, but without sin, thank God. Yes, there are many fun things on this earth to do that are not sinful. "Is it possible to live a life without sin?" Yes, Jesus would not have told us to repent if it could not be done. It is done through Jesus and the renewing of the mind.

Romans 12:2 (ESV)

² Do not be conformed to this world, but be transformed by the renewal of your mind, that by testing you may discern what is the will of God, what is good and acceptable and perfect.

2 Corinthians 5:17 (NIV)

¹⁷ Therefore, if anyone is in Christ, the new creation has come: The old has gone, the new is here!

Philippians 4:13 (ESV)

¹³ I can do all things through him who strengthens me.

God tells us in many different ways and in many verses that we are to repent. The verses in this book about repenting are just a few of the many verses in the Bible on the subject. God also tells us how to repent. "Do not be conformed to this world;" do not continue to live a lifestyle of sin. "Be transformed by the renewing of your mind;" you transform yourself by renewing your mind with what God tells you to do and what not to do in the Bible. The way you become a new creation is to choose not to do sinful things in your life. Stop dwelling on the things that cause you to sin. "The new is here." You need to make an effort to live a life without sin. You can do this with the help of the Holy Spirit; you do not have to do it on your own.

By ourselves, it is impossible to live a life without sin, but with Christ, nothing is impossible; by conforming ourselves to His Word, we can live a life without sin. Do not try to live your Christian life on your own; it will not work. Do it with Christ; talk to Him every day. Pray to God every day. God is your Father. Jesus is your brother, your friend, and your personal Savior. God and Jesus want a personal relationship with you. "Who? Me?" Yes! You! God, Jesus, and the Holy Spirit love you so much that They want a personal relationship with you, to be with you forever. God loves you. Jesus loves you. The Holy Spirit loves you. The Holy Spirit is your helper, comforter, and counselor. They all three love you. Jesus and the Holy Spirit will help you to stop sinning every day of your life. Remember, God so loved the world (God so loved the people), God so loved you that He gave you His Son, Jesus Christ. Are you important to God? Yes, you are so important to God that He gave you His Son.

In Matthew 16:24–25 (ESV), Jesus said,

[24] Then Jesus told his disciples, "If anyone would come after me, let him deny himself and take up his cross and follow me.

[25] For whoever would save his life will lose it, but whoever loses his life for my sake will find it.

The same of what is being said is also found in the Gospel of Matthew 10:38-39, Mark 8:34-35, and Luke 9:23-24. I want to point out that some translations will say "good news" instead of "the gospel." The phrase "good news" is another way of saying "the gospel."

Jesus also said in John 12:25 (ESV),

²⁵ Whoever loves his life loses it, and whoever hates his life in this world will keep it for eternal life.

These verses from Matthew, Mark, Luke, and John are saying the same thing about losing and finding your life, and they are all tied in with repenting. Jesus is saying several things in these verses. In Matthew, He is saying that if we do not change our ways, we are not worthy of Him. Then in all four Gospels, Jesus is talking about clinging to or living our life in this world. In other words, if we continue to live a sinful life, we will lose our eternal life. We will keep our eternal life in heaven only if we (lose) turn away from the things that we know are sinful in our earthly life.

Jesus died on the cross for us. When He said, "Take up your cross and follow Me," what He meant was to die to yourself. To die to yourself is to quit living for yourself and to start living for God. This will not happen to you overnight. It is a process to change your life for God. If you do not start to change, then you need to check your heart to see if you really want a close walk with Jesus.

Right now, we are talking about repenting, changing our minds, and turning away from our sinful lives. To keep your life is to live *without* God, Jesus, and the Holy Spirit and to do sinful things, which will lead you to hell. Do the right thing. Start by not continuing to do the sinful things in your life. It is a struggle, but with the help of Jesus and the Holy Spirit, it can be done.

"But, Mike, how do I follow Jesus?" By reading and studying the Bible, praying to God, and going to a church that preaches what is in the scriptures of the Bible. By doing the things that God and Jesus tell us to do in the Bible.

From my past experience, the more I seek God's will in my life, the easier it is to overcome sin. Also, do not be just a Sunday born-again believer. Being a born-again Christian is an everyday occurrence for the rest of your life. Obey God's commands that are in the Bible. Do not continue to do or practice things that are not in the Bible or do not lineup with the Bible. Through reading and studying the Bible, you will really get to know God the Father, God the Son, and God the Holy Spirit. Also, by praying and worshipping God for more than one hour a week. Talk to God; He wants to have a personal relationship with you.

We need to deny ourselves and follow Jesus. Jesus gave His life for us so that we could have a way to go to heaven. Jesus is life. Follow Jesus Christ, the Son of God; you will have everlasting life in heaven.

"What will or would happen to me if I do not take up my cross and follow Jesus?" Let's first talk about what happens if you do follow Jesus. You will live a life of getting to know Almighty God, the creator of heaven and Earth, and Jesus Christ, His Son, who loves you dearly. All with the help of the Holy Spirit, who lives in you. You will live your life free from the sinful things that previously controlled you. You will still have fun in life but without sin. You will find out that you will be able to express yourself without foul language, and people will still understand that you mean what you are saying. You will have your ups and downs in life, and God will be with you all the time, through the good times and the bad. Just as God gives you peace of mind in the good times, so will He give you peace of mind in the bad times because you can turn to God and trust that He will help you through them.

"Mike, do you have any fun in your life?" Yes, and without the sinful things this world has to offer. I also have a joy in my heart that cannot be explained. I do not have a single drop of alcohol in me, and I am not on any drugs. I have not done any of that since 1972, thank God. But I started to laugh really hard as I write about the joy of the Lord because God has refilled me with His joy. It is great! Let God be the Lord of your life in everything that you do, and you, too, can have this joy. Now, let me come down back to Earth, so I can finish what I am writing. God and Jesus can give you a joy in your heart like nothing else can. You do not get this joy overnight, and it is not constant because life does have its ups and downs.

Oh! Did I mention after all that has been said and done, the ups and downs, the good times and the bad, if you have taken up your cross and followed Jesus, that when your physical body dies, your spirit will go to heaven and you will live happily ever after with God, Jesus, and the Holy Spirit?

Now, to answer your question, what will happen if you do not take up your cross and follow Jesus? You will live a life of ups and downs, good times and bad times, but without God or Jesus in your life, you will never experience the joy of the Lord. You will continue to live a life with sin in it. You will say, "I am good," "I do good things," "I am not a bad person." Even though this is true, you will not be forgiven of your sins, and after all that has been said and done, Jesus will say, "23 I never knew you; depart from me, you workers of lawlessness" (Matthew 7:23, ESV). You will not live happily ever after in heaven. According to the Bible, sin is sin. No matter how good you are, you still have sinned, and being good is not enough because, according to God, sin separates us from Him. So now that you are saved, take up your cross and follow Jesus. Remember, God the Father, God the Son (Jesus), and God the Holy Spirit will always, and I mean will always, love you. They want a personal relationship with you!

I have heard, "Once saved, always saved." This may or may not be true, and it is not a license to sin. I have heard good arguments from both sides of this, but why take the chance? After reading what we have read, do you want to take the chance and maybe get into heaven by the skin of your teeth or risk not getting into heaven? But just because a person sins after being born again, it does not mean that the person has lost their salvation. It took me four years to get swearing out of my vocabulary. When I swore, I did not lose my salvation, but I did show God disrespect. If you sin after being born again, you do not lose your salvation, but it is not good to continue in sin because of all the warnings in the Bible. Yes, we have 1 John 1:9, but do you want to continuously show God that you do not love Him? Read John 14:15 again. "If you love Me, keep My commandments." Some Christians believe that once saved, always saved, and some Christians do not believe that once saved, always saved. I will leave that one up to you because I want all Christians to use this book to help others.

Sin separates us from God, so repent and turn away from sin. Do your best to live a life free from sin. If you do sin, you have an advocate, Jesus Christ. You can go to Jesus, and He will forgive you of your sins.

"Mike, does the Bible say swearing is a sin?" I will answer that question in the next chapter.

CHAPTER 11:

WHAT IS SIN?

Sin is being disobedient to God. When we disobey God's commands and commandments, we are sinning against God. In many ways, people live a lifestyle of sin and don't think that they are sinning against God. It seems like people think because their lifestyle is common and accepted by society today, that it should not be considered a sin by God anymore. They think He should be okay with how they live. Just because certain sins are accepted by law as a lifestyle and it is okay by or with society, this does not mean it is no longer a sin to God.

"Mike, you talked of swearing as being a sin. You said it took you four years to get swearing out of your vocabulary. Does the Bible say swearing is a sin?" Yes, by our own definitions of swearing, the Bible says swearing is a sin.

It is said that the Bible does not say swearing is a sin. This is because no one has taken the time to look at the definitions of swearing according to the Bible. According to our definitions, the Bible does say swearing is a sin. The Bible describes bad language as being corrupt communication and strongly says we should not have corrupt communication coming out of our mouths. We know corrupt things are sinful. Without using the word "swear" or "swearing," the Bible says swearing is a sin. We describe our swear words the same way the Bible describes corrupt communications. Let us look at what we define swearing as. Swearing is saying bad words or saying what we consider filthy words. We define some swear words as a phrase of profanity or, as some would say, obscene words to the ears. Using God and Jesus or Jesus Christ without talking about them or using their names with swear words is blasphemy. Swearing is a foul, strong, filthy language. These are the definitions that we give for our swear words. Swear words have never been considered good words to use. People use swear words to express themselves when they are angry or when they want others to know they mean it. People use them when telling a filthy joke. We often say, "A person has a filthy mouth when they say a lot of swear words." We tell our children not to say swear words because they are filthy. Swearing is profane, obscene, foul, and filthy language, according to our definitions.

Matthew 12:34 (ESV)

[34] You brood of vipers! How can you speak good, when you are evil? For out of the abundance of the heart the mouth speaks.

Ephesians 4:29 (KJV)

[29] Let no corrupt communication proceed out of your mouth, but that which is good to the use of edifying, that it may minister grace unto the hearers.

Colossians 3:8 (KJV)

[8] But now ye also put off all these; anger, wrath, malice, blasphemy, filthy communication out of your mouth.

James 3:10 (KJV)

¹⁰ Out of the same mouth proceedeth blessing and cursing. My brethren, these things ought not so to be.

Matthew 12:34 says, "³⁴ For out of the abundance of the heart the mouth speaks."

Our heart cannot be right with God if we are speaking foul, filthy swear words, for out of the abundance of the heart, the mouth speaks. We tell our children not to say that swear word or this swear word because they are filthy. When someone says swear words, we say, "Oh, what a filthy mouth." Some people will say, "And they eat with that mouth?" Some say, "Pardon my French."

Let's look at certain parts of these verses. Ephesians 4:29, "Let no corrupt communication proceed or corrupting talk come out of your mouths." Colossians 3:8, "But now you must put away filthy communication or obscene talk from your mouth." James 3:10, "From the same mouth proceeds or come blessing and cursing. My brother, these things ought not to be so."

These verses say corrupt, cursing, and filthy communications should not come out of our mouths, letting us know this is sin. We consider and define swear words as filthy language in our communications. We define swear words as a filthy language of communication. The Bible says we should not have filthy communication coming out of our mouths. Therefore, by our definitions of swear words and according to the Bible, swearing is a sin.

There is one more thing about swearing. God has more than one name. God's names are not filthy, but when people use His names to express themselves or use His names with swear words, it is swearing. When people use His names without talking about Him, it is swearing. It is taking His name in vain. Read Exodus 20:7 and Deuteronomy 5:11.

There are many sins that separate us from God. The following verses name sins that keep people from inheriting the kingdom of God.

1 Corinthians 6:9 (KJV)

⁹ Know ye not that the unrighteous shall not inherit the kingdom of God? Be not deceived: neither fornicators, nor idolaters, nor adulterers, nor effeminate, nor abusers of themselves with mankind.

1 Timothy 1:10 (ESV)

¹⁰ The sexually immoral, men who practice homosexuality, enslavers, liars, perjurers, and whatever else is contrary to sound doctrine.

Revelation 21:8 (KJV)

⁸ But the fearful, and unbelieving, and the abominable, and murderers, and whoremongers, and sorcerers, and idolaters, and all liars, shall have their part in the lake which burneth with fire and brimstone: which is the second death.

Galatians 5:19–21 (KJV)

¹⁹ Now the works of the flesh are manifest, which are these; Adultery, fornication, uncleanness, lasciviousness,

²⁰ Idolatry, witchcraft, hatred, variance, emulations, wrath, strife, seditions, heresies,

²¹ Envyings, murders, drunkenness, revellings, and such like: of the which I tell you before, as I have also told you in time past, that they which do such things shall not inherit the kingdom of God.

These verses clearly state that the people committing these sins will not inherit the kingdom of God. If any of these verses offend someone because they mention their lifestyle, then they have to take it up with God. I know I am repeating this, but just because certain sins have become an acceptable common lifestyle by law and society, that does not mean that God no longer considers them to be sins.

"How do I overcome sin?" You asked a very good question. Since Adam and Eve bit the apple, Satan and his demons have been practicing to tempt us. They are very clever in tempting us to sin. It takes practice for us to overcome sin. It is not easy for everyone to overcome sin right away, but we still need to strive to live a life without sin. Jesus was tempted just like us.

Hebrews 4:14–15 (KJV)

¹⁴ Seeing then that we have a great high priest, that is passed into the heavens, Jesus the Son of God, let us hold fast our profession.

¹⁵ For we have not an high priest which cannot be touched with the feeling of our infirmities; but was in all points tempted like as we are, yet without sin.

In verse 14, Jesus is our high priest. In verse 15, we see He was tempted in every way as we are, but He did not sin. Therefore, a temptation of thought or a temptation of physical sight is not a sin. If it were then Jesus would not be without sin. "Mike, when does a temptation of thought or a temptation of physical sight become sin?" It becomes sin when we accept the temptation by giving it a place in our mind and in our heart by focusing on it and starting to think of doing whatever the temptation is. It becomes sin by thinking and dwelling on what we thought or saw.

Let's see what Jesus did when He was confronted with temptation. If you open your Bible and read Matthew 4:1–11 or Luke 4:3–13, they speak of three things that Jesus was tempted with by Satan. In each temptation, Jesus answered him with what is written in the Word. This is one of the reasons why I keep telling you to read your Bible so you know what's written in order to stand on it in times of battle. We have to assume that Jesus was tempted many other times because He was tempted in every way that we are.

Jesus did not focus on the temptations placed before Him. We need to be attentive to follow what He did because when we focus on the temptation before us, we are yielding to our fleshly desires and committing the sin in our heart. The more we apply the Word to our thoughts and actions, the less we want to sin. This makes it easier to not yield to the temptation.

When sinful thoughts attack, fight back with Scripture. Do not dwell on the sin. You can resist the temptations of the devil by refusing to accept them and by being a doer of the Word. Resisting temptation is a fight. Using the following two verses can help you overcome temptation. There are many other verses as well.

Philippians 4:13 (KJV)

¹³ I can do all things through Christ which strengthenth me.

First John 5:4 (KJV)

⁴ For whatsoever is born of God overcometh the world: and this is the victory that overcometh the world, even our faith."

You can say, "I can overcome this temptation because I am an overcomer of the world, and I can do all things through Christ who strengthens me." Professing and believing this will help you to overcome the temptations.

James 4:7 (KJV)

⁷ Submit yourselves therefore to God. Resist the devil, and he will flee from you.

Resist the devil, and he will flee from you. This does not mean you are being tempted directly by Satan. Why? Because Satan is not omnipresent, he cannot be everywhere at once like God can, so he needs demons to help him tempt people to sin. Satan himself cannot tempt everyone in the world at the same time. When we submit ourselves to God and resist the devil, we are acting on the Word. If we are diligent in resisting his temptations, Satan will flee from us. This does not mean that we will never be tempted by him or his demons again. Satan, with the help of his demons, will try again and again to tempt us to commit sin. Some sins have a stronghold on people's lives, and that can make it harder for them to quit doing them at first. Just like God puts thoughts in our minds to do good things, Satan and demons can put thoughts in our minds to tempt us to commit sin.

With all the bad things that are happening in the world today, we can see that a lot of unbelievers are listening to Satan or demons. They think they are acting on their own thoughts and ideas. They do not know, nor have any idea, that they are listening to Satan or demons and that it is the sin in their lives that is sending them to hell. They have no idea that they are being deceived. If they die *before* they receive Jesus as Lord and Savior, they will have lost the spiritual battle.

At one time or another, a believer will fall into temptation and sin. When this happens, it does not mean the person is not a doer of the Word. No one is perfect, and even a strong believer can fall or yield to temptation. But a doer of the Word does not continue to live a sinful life. They strive to live a life without sin.

Some of the things that are sinful to God are to practice and believe in religious rituals that are not in the Bible. It is also a sin to believe in spiritual things that are not in the Bible and that contradict the Bible. Now the question is, why are these things a sin to God? Because it is the same as saying we do not believe in the inspired written Word of God. This is another reason why it is important to read your Bible. When we submit ourselves to God, it becomes easy to resist the temptation of sin. Remember, the Holy Spirit and Jesus Christ can help you overcome the sins in your life. When you repent, God will forgive you.

I must say, just because a person is born again and is striving to live a life without sin, it does not mean that person will not sin again. No one is perfect.

CHAPTER 12:

A New Creature in Christ

Now we know without any doubt that we are to repent of all sin; it is a must; it is not an option. We must repent and turn away from sin.

Side note: For all the people who believe that Christ is Jesus' last name, I have to say it is not. In my research, I found the word "Christ" is one of Jesus' titles. Christ has several meanings here are some of them. It comes from the Greek word *Christos*. It means Jesus is the anointed one, the Messiah, the chosen one by God to be a king and a deliverer. When you see the name Jesus Christ or Christ Jesus, Christ is not His last name but the title of who He is to us.

Romans 6:6-7 (NIV)

⁶ For we know our old self was crucified with him so that the body ruled by sin might be done away with, that we should no longer be slaves to sin—

⁷ because anyone who has died has been freed from sin.

2 Corinthians 5:17 (NIV)

¹⁷ Therefore, if anyone is in Christ, the new creation is come: The old has gone, the new is here!

As we just read in these verses, we see our old sinful self was crucified with Jesus; therefore, we no longer are slaves to sin. We are now new creatures in Christ. Spiritually speaking, our sinful bodies were crucified with Christ Jesus. Therefore, we are to crucify the old man that is in us, which is our sinful nature. In a sense, our old man is the sins that we do or did in life, whether big or small. We must spiritually crucify (kill) the old man in us. This means to turn away from sin by lining up our will with God's will. Stop doing sinful things in your life. Ask Jesus and the Holy Spirit to help you. Do not be afraid to ask for help. Like I said before, God, Jesus, and the Holy Spirit always have time for you. They are waiting with open arms to help you.

"Is there anything else that God wants me to do?" I am so glad that you asked that question. The answer is yes.

Let's look at Romans 12:1-3 (ESV),

¹ I appeal to you therefore, brothers, by the mercies of God, to present your bodies as a living sacrifice, holy and acceptable to God, which is your spiritual worship.

² Do not be conformed to this world, but be transformed by the renewal of your mind, that by testing you may discern what is the will of God, what is good and acceptable and perfect.

³ For by grace given to me I say to everyone among you not to think of himself more highly than he ought to think, but to think with sober judgment,

each according to the measure of faith that God has assigned.

"Mike, how do we do all that?" That is a very good question. I am glad you asked. Start to read the Bible every day. This is how you renew your mind. Read it at your own pace, and think about what you have read. Remember, you are not just reading any book, but it is God's written Word. It is what God wants you to know and do. It is history. It tells you exactly how God wants you to live. Start by reading the New Testament. "Why read the New Testament first?" Because it is God's new covenant with man, which is God's covenant with us today. Yes, there are things in the Old Testament that still apply to us today. My suggestion is to read in this order: first, the Gospel of John, then read Galatians, Ephesians, Philippians, and Colossians, and then read 1 and 2 Corinthians. After reading these books you should be ready to read the books 1 John, Acts, and Romans. All of these books will help you become strong in your Christian walk in life.

When you have read at least these books in the New Testament, you will then know enough of what God expects of you to start reading books out of the Old Testament. I am not saying that you cannot read anything out of the Old Testament before you finish these books; you can. It is just that I know these books will help you to become a strong Christian. One of your goals in life should be to read the whole Bible. For those who have never read the Bible, get a Bible that is easy for you to read and understand. The table of contents will tell you where each book is in the Bible. For example, when you see John 3:16, the name John is the book in the Bible. The number before the colon is the chapter, and the number after the colon is the verse in that chapter. The chapter number is always a little bigger than the verse number in the Bible.

When you read the Bible, you are renewing your mind. Let God's Word, the Bible, change your way of thinking. Do not think of yourself as better than someone else. We are all created equal, not physically but spiritually. Love everyone. You can hate what they do but never hate the person. Some people will say, "Oh, you're one of those 'love them but hate what they do.'" Well, I sure am not going to love the bad things that people do. No matter how bad a person may be, you should still love them. But it is all right to hate the bad and sinful things they do. Does God love what a sinner does? No. God hates sin. God definitely hates sin, but He loves the sinners. Yes! "For God so love the world (sinners) that He gave His Son." To give each and every one of us a chance to go to heaven. Matthew 5:44 says to love your enemies.

Romans 12:2 (NLT), "2 Don't copy the behavior and customs of this world, but let God transform you." What God is saying is, stop living a life of sin and live the way He wants you to live. The only way to do that is to obey God's commands. His commands are in the Bible. The following statement is worth repeating: being born again is not being religious as to being holier than thou or acting holier than thou when you are with unbelievers. It is doing what the Word of God tells us to do. Repenting is not the only way of loving God. Let us look at some other ways.

God gives each one of us the same measure of faith. "Mike, why do some people seem to have more faith than others if God gives each of us the same measure of faith? Can we ask for more faith?" No. They really don't have more faith; they have stronger faith. The faith that God gives us is all that we need. It's like a muscle that needs to be developed. If you exercise, you will have stronger muscles than those who don't. If others exercise more than you, they will have stronger muscles. Faith is the same way. Those who exercise their faith have a stronger faith. The only way to have strong faith is to exercise it. Just like a muscle, you start with small things and work your way up to the big things. You have to start believing God for the little things in life first before you can believe God for the big things in life. And that is how you exercise and build up your faith. Let's move on.

Proverbs 2:1-2 (ESV)

[1] My son, if you receive my words and treasure up my commandments with you, [2] making your ear attentive to wisdom and inclining your heart to understanding.

Proverbs 3:1-2 (ESV)

[1] My son, do not forget my teaching, but let your heart keep my commandments, [2] for length of days and years of life and peace they will add to you.

Proverbs 4:20-22 (ESV),

[20] My son, be attentive to my words; incline your ear to my sayings.

[21] Let them not escape from your sight; keep them within your heart.

[22] For they are life to those who find them, and healing to all their flesh.

God is telling you to attend to His words. Put them deep in your heart. Store His commands deep in your heart. Consent and submit to His sayings, His commands, His words. "How do you get them into your heart?" Through memorization, meditation, and personalization. By reading the Bible over and over, again and again, God will be able to put His commands deep in your heart. Do not let God's Word depart from your sight; by doing this, you will live many years (Proverbs 3:2). God's Word will bring health to your flesh. God wants you to read and study His Word. This will help you to know what God's will is for you. Also, reading and studying the Bible will help you build your relationship with God. The biggest part of having a personal relationship with God, Jesus Christ, and the Holy Spirit is by doing the Word, putting what it teaches into practice, and also by praying and talking to God every day. You cannot be a doer of the Word if you do not read it.

Romans 12:2 tells us to renew our minds.

Proverbs 4:23–27 (ESV)

[23] Keep your heart with all vigilance, for from it flow the springs of life.

[24] Put away from you crooked speech, and put devious talk far from you.

[25] Let your eyes look directly forward, and your gaze be straight before you.

[26] Ponder the path of your feet; then all your ways will be sure.

[27] Do not swerve to the right or to the left; turn your foot away from evil.

You guard your heart by not letting your mind dwell on evil desires. Watch how you talk. Get rid of perverse talking. Do not look at the past, but look at what God has for you. Get yourself right with God, and do not let evil things keep you from doing good. Again, be a doer of God's Word. The Holy Spirit will help you. You do not have to do it by yourself. The Holy Spirit is in you and is always there to help you to do the right thing. For support, go to a Bible-believing church where the people are born again.

God and Jesus want to be first in your life. It is only right that They hold that place. After all, God created you, and Jesus died on the cross for you and has purchased eternal life for you.

Matthew 6:33 (ESV)

[33] But seek first the kingdom of God and his righteousness, and all those things will be added to you.

"Mike, how do I seek first the kingdom of God in my life?" Go to church at least once a week and worship God. Do not make a lot of plans that will make you miss church a lot. Read your Bible every day and study it. Pray to God and Jesus every day. You can talk to God, Jesus, and the Holy Spirit whenever you want because They always have time for you, and They are never, ever too busy for you. Before you make plans in your life, ask God what He wants you to do. Always ask God to help you when making big decisions in your life. God will help you. As you grow in the Lord, you will start to know when He is telling you things.

When you go on vacation, and you are away from your home on a Sunday, find a church in the area and go to it. Never take a vacation from God. Include God in your everyday life. After all, He is now your Father and is with you always. God cares about your every need in life. As Jesus said, if you seek the kingdom of God first, He will give you all your needs. In other words, put God and Jesus first in your life, before everything else, then all of your needs will be given to you. But first you have to put God first in your life, in everything that you say and do. Be a doer of the Word. Make sure that what you are being shown from the Bible is correct; check it out. Check me out. Make sure I am talking about what the verses are talking about. Do as I do and use more than just one translation of the Bible; this way, you will get a better understanding of the Bible.

Remember, if your doctrinal beliefs do not line up with the rest of the verses in the Bible, your doctrinal beliefs are wrong. God has placed in the Bible everything that we are to believe. God did not leave anything out. If you believe a doctrine just because it makes sense, but it does not line up with the rest of the verses, then it is wrong. For example, the saying, "God helps those who help themselves." That is not in the Bible; it is not biblical at all. God does help us and give us things, not because we help ourselves, but because we believe, trust, and have faith in Him and because He loves us.

The following is for those who think they can just wait for God, and He will give them things. Even though He does help us and gives us things, that does not mean we can sit in our seats all day and wait for God to give us everything on a silver platter. We still have to do our part as well. Just like an earthly parent, God does not always give us what we want.

In the last part of the verse in Mark 12:28, Jesus was asked what is the first or greatest commandment. Jesus gives the answer in verse 30.

> Mark 12:28–31 (ESV)
>
> [28] And one of the scribes came up and heard them disputing with one another, and seeing that he answered them well, asked him, "Which commandment is the most important of all?"
>
> [29] Jesus answered, "The most important is, 'Hear, O Israel: The Lord our God, the Lord is one.
>
> [30] And you shall love the Lord your God with all your heart and with all your soul and with all your mind and with all your strength.'
>
> [31] The second is this: 'You shall love your neighbor as yourself.' There is no other commandment greater than these."

Jesus is not giving us a new commandment here. He is quoting and referring to scriptures in Deuteronomy. When you love someone with all your heart, soul, mind, and strength, you usually have a very strong personal relationship with that person. God wants a very strong personal relationship with you. This means talking to God every day and including God in everything you do. Do not just go to church on Sundays and then forget about God the rest of the week. That is not a strong personal relationship with God. Would you like it if someone that you loved dearly and is with you constantly would pay tribute to you for one hour a week and forget about you until that hour comes up in the next week? That is what a lot of church-going people do unless they have a strong personal relationship with God. God really wants more than one hour a week with you. God wants to have time with you every day of your life.

God loves you so much that you can have a regular conversation with Him. "Well, I never hear God talk to me." Yes, it is true a lot of times we do not hear God but you will eventually learn and know when God is speaking to you or when He puts thoughts into your mind. At first, you may not recognize when God is talking to you. God hardly ever talks to us in an audible voice. God speaks to us in many different ways. Not always in the way we think or are looking for. He will talk to us through the Bible a lot. A verse or verses will, in a sense, jump out at us, like, wow, this is what I am supposed to do or not do, or believe or not believe. He will talk to us through people, and they will not always know that God is talking to us through them. God definitely talks to us in church through the sermons.

I do not know how to explain it to you, but I just know when God is talking to me. If you do not have a strong personal relationship with God, you may not always know when He is talking to you. I have to admit I do not hear God every day. Most Christians do not hear God all the time, but we know when our thoughts come from God because they line up with the Bible. God talks to us all the time, but we don't always listen.

What is said or written in Mark 12:28–31 can also be found in Matthew 22:36–40 and in Luke 10:25–28. When Jesus was speaking of the first, most important, and greatest commandment, I know He was referring to verses in Deuteronomy because of how He worded His response.

Deuteronomy 6:4–6 (NLT)

⁴ Listen, O Israel! The LORD is our God, the LORD alone.

⁵ And you must love the LORD your God with all your heart, all your soul, and all your strength.

⁶ And you must commit yourselves wholeheartedly to these commands that I am giving you today.

Deuteronomy 10:12 (NIV)

¹² And now, Israel, what does the LORD your God ask of you but to fear the LORD your God, to walk in obedience to him, to love him, to serve the LORD your God with all your heart and with all your soul.

(These two commandants are not part of the ten commandants.)

Jesus said that we, you and I, are to love God with all our heart. You are to love the Lord your God with all your mind, and you are to love God with all your strength. In other words, you are to love God with everything you've got. Give God all your love, for He has given you all His love through Jesus Christ, His Son, our Savior. Yes, you can still have fun in life, but do not forget about God in doing so. God does not want just a one-hour-a-week relationship with you. He wants your love and a relationship with you on a day-to-day basis. You do not have to be holier than thou to have a relationship with God.

A person will say: I love football, I love basketball, I love to dance, I love that movie, I love to play video games, I love texting, I love music, and the list is endless. Nine times out of ten, when people say they love something, they usually mean it and/or they really get into it. But do you love God and Jesus that same way? When you go to church, do you really show God and Jesus your love and really get into it? Do you really think about and feel your love for God and Jesus when you are in church? Do you think of how much God and Jesus love you and what Jesus went through for you? Do you really get into the message that is being preached that Sunday, or do you just go, listen, and wonder when church will be over? Only you, God, Jesus, and the Holy Spirit know the answers to these questions.

God and Jesus love you very much, and They are a forgiving God. I love You, God. Think about it. That was easy to say. I love You, God. When you said, "I love You, God," did you feel in your heart, mind, and soul the love that you have for God, or did you just say, "I love You, God"? Do you think of God every day? Do you thank God each day for the things that He has done for you, and are you grateful for what He has done? Do you tell God, "I love You," more than once a week? Again, only you, God, Jesus, and the Holy Spirit know the answers to these questions. Love God and Jesus today. Be thankful and grateful to Him. No matter what, God always loves you.

Before we start on the second command, let's read once more the first command; "You shall love the Lord your God with all your heart and with all your soul and with all your mind and with all your strength."

The second command is to love your neighbor as yourself. As hard as it is for us, because of various reasons, God still wants us to love our neighbors. These two commands are God's greatest commandments.

Note: Back in Jesus' and the apostle's days, the Old Testament was not called the Old Testament, because the New Testament was not written yet. At that time, there was no one name for the Old Testament. It was called or referred to as the Pentateuch, the Torah, the Law and the Prophets, or the Scriptures.

The second commandment that Jesus is referring to is in Leviticus, the second half of the verse.

Leviticus 19:18 (NLT)

18 But love your neighbor as yourself. I am the LORD.

Love. Yes, we are to love our neighbors even though we may not like what they do or believe. You can hate what they do or believe, but you are to still love them. You are to love your neighbor even if they do not believe what you believe. You do not have to agree with them, but you are to still love them. Romans 12:18 (NIV), "18 If it is possible, as far as it depends on you, live at peace with everyone." Be a doer of the Word. Jesus said, "If you love Me, you will keep My commandments." We have just read of His two greatest commands…practice them.

In Deuteronomy 6:6 (NLT), we read, "6 And you must commit yourselves wholeheartedly to these commands that I am giving you today." God wants us to love Him with all our heart. Remember what Jesus did for you. He loves you. Be all you can be for God. Does God want you to have fun in life? Yes, but without sin. Remember what we read in Romans 6:23, that the wages of sin is death. "What is this death, if people sin all the time and they are still alive? If people are still alive after they sinned, then what kind of death are we talking about?" Those are two excellent questions.

Genesis 2:17 (NIV)

¹⁷ But you must not eat from the tree of the knowledge of good and evil, for when you eat from it you will certainly die.

Adam and Eve were told not to eat from the tree of knowledge of good and evil because they would die if they did. Did Adam and Eve physically die right away when they ate from the tree of knowledge? No, they were still alive, but they did die spiritually. The moment they ate from the tree of knowledge of good and evil, they died spiritually right away. Why? Because they disobeyed God when they ate of the tree of knowledge. When they disobeyed God, they sinned against Him and became spiritually dead. It is because of sin that we were born spiritually dead, and that is why God considers our spirit dead before we accept Jesus Christ as our Savior.

When we receive Jesus Christ as our Savior, our spirit becomes alive; this is what Jesus calls being born again. When our spirit is dead because of sin, we are separated from God. When we are separated from God, we are going to hell, not heaven, because separation from God is spiritual death. After we receive Jesus Christ as our Savior and repent, our Spirit becomes alive, and we are no longer separated from God, and we are now going to heaven.

1 Corinthians 15:22 (NIV)

²² For as in Adam all die [because we all belong to Adam], so in Christ all will be made alive [now belonging to Christ].

When Adam sinned, it separated not only him but all of us from God because we all belong to Adam. When we accepted Jesus Christ as our personal Savior, Jesus brought us back to God. Now, we no longer belong to Adam, but rather, we belong to Jesus Christ. Christ is the bridge back to God for us. In Christ, we are no longer separated from God. Keep your spirit alive and live for God and for Jesus Christ. Keep your spirit alive every day of your life by renewing your mind with the Word of God. On the day of judgment, you will be glad you did. Love God with all your heart, with all your mind, with all your strength, and with all your soul, for He is right there with you all the time. God loves you. Yes! God loves you! The Holy Spirit dwells in you. Start showing your love for God by being a doer of the Word. Remember, when one becomes born again, the Holy Spirit comes and dwells in them. If you are born again, the Holy Spirit is dwelling in you right now. When you repent of your sins, turn away from them, and stop doing them, you are showing God that you love Him.

Repenting is a part of loving God and Jesus, "If you love Me, you will keep (obey) My commandments." I have one more thing I want to say about sin and repenting, but I want to say it at the end of chapter 15 because it ties in with Jesus being our advocate.

Here is a short list of verses to look up that God considers us to be once we are born again. You can personalize them and confess these in the first person (I am) to build up your spirit and faith as a new creature in Christ.

> I am justified by faith and I am at peace with God through our Lord Jesus Christ (Romans 5:1).

I am free from the law of sin and death (Romans 8:2).

I am adopted by God, having received the Spirit of adoption, and God is my Father (Romans 8:15).

I am a joint-heir with Christ (Romans 8:17).

I am led by the Spirit of God, and I am a child of God (Romans 8:14, 16).

I am greatly loved by God (John 3:16; Romans 1:7).

I am God's temple and God's Spirit dwells in me (1 Corinthians 3:16).

I am washed, sanctified, and justified in the name of the Lord Jesus, and by the Spirit of God (1 Corinthians 6:11).

I am a new creation in Christ (2 Corinthians 5:17).

I am an ambassador for Christ (2 Corinthians 5:20).

I am the righteousness of God in Christ (2 Corinthians 5:21).

I am holy and without blame before Him in love (Ephesians 1:4; 1 Peter 1:16).

I am forgiven of all my sins and washed in the blood (Ephesians 1:7).

I am raised up with Him and seated with Him in the heavenly places in Christ Jesus (Ephesians 2:6).

I am His workmanship, created in Christ Jesus for good works, which God prepared beforehand, that I should walk in them (Ephesians 2:10).

> I am redeemed through Jesus' blood, for the forgiveness of sins (Colossians 1:14).
>
> I am a chosen race, a royal priesthood, a holy nation, a people for His own possession, that I may proclaim the excellences of Him (1 Peter 2:9).
>
> I am forgiven of sins and cleansed from all unrighteousness (1 John 1:9).
>
> I am more than a conqueror through Him who loved us (Romans 8:37).

According to God, you are all of this and more the moment you are born again. Confessing these scriptures and others like these will help you to know who you are as a new creature in Jesus Christ. They will also help you in resisting temptation.

Before moving on, I want to clear up any confusion I may have created for anyone on a few things. Jesus did do some things on a physical level, which affected a spiritual level. All of what Jesus went through to die on the cross and rise from the dead was on a physical level, which affected a spiritual level. The spiritual level that was affected is that now our spirits are alive and have a way to heaven. Jesus did not save our physical bodies from dying; He saved our spirits from dying a spiritual death. Through His physical act of dying and rising from the dead, we have been saved from an eternal death in hell to an eternal life with Christ.

In Mark 16:19, Luke 24:50–51, and Acts 1:1–11, Jesus went to heaven in a physical body, not a spiritual one; a physical level that affected a spiritual level. Now, the Holy Spirit can come and dwell in our bodies with us.

"Mike, what is this spiritual death that lasts forever in hell that Jesus saved us from?" Your question will be answered in the next chapter.

CHAPTER 13:

WHAT DID JESUS SAVE US FROM?

What did Jesus save us from? He saved us from sin and death in hell. In Matthew and Luke, Jesus talks a little bit about two gates, one that leads to hell and one that leads to heaven. Jesus Himself spoke these words.

> Matthew 7:13–14 (NIV)
>
> [13] Enter through the narrow gate. For wide is the gate and broad is the road that leads to destruction [hell], and many enter through it.
>
> [14] But small is the gate and narrow the road that leads to life, and only a few find it.

> Luke 13:23–24 (NIV)
>
> [23] Someone asked him, "Lord, are only a few people going to be saved?" He said to them,
>
> [24] "Make every effort to enter through the narrow door, because many, I tell you, will try to enter and will not be able to."

1 Timothy 6:12 (NIV)

¹² Fight the good fight of the faith. Take hold of the eternal life to which you were called when you made your good confession in the presence of many witnesses.

Yes! Jesus is the only way, the gate to heaven. We are saved through Him by the shedding of His blood, His death on the cross, and by His resurrection.

Jesus is talking about the gate to hell and the gate to heaven. He said many people are going to hell, and only a few are going to heaven. Jesus said to strive and make every effort to enter heaven, for many will try to enter, but few will make it. If you will notice, Jesus Himself said the gateway to hell is wide, and the gateway to heaven is narrow because many people are going to hell, and few people are going to heaven. Why? Because few will accept Jesus as their personal Savior and commit themselves to repent and being a good witness for God.

If everyone were going to heaven, then Jesus would not have made these statements. Jesus made it very clear that a lot of people are going to hell. God wants everyone to go to heaven, but He wants us to come to Him of our own free will. God gave us the right to choose which way we will go. If God were to choose our way for us, then He would be guilty of taking away our free will to choose. In a sense, God would be going against His will if He made the choice for us to go to heaven.

Unfortunately, a lot of us make the wrong choice. One of the problems is people think, *I am a good person, I'm going to heaven, I don't really need to go to church,* or they think everyone is going to heaven. If God could have His way, everyone would be a good person and be on their way to heaven. God cannot and will not go against His own Word. There is one thing that God is not getting His own way in, and that is not everyone is going to heaven. Remember, Jesus Himself said few will find their way into heaven. God cannot force us to go to heaven. In 1 Corinthians, Paul gives us a small list of just some of the sinful behaviors that will cause a person to not go to heaven.

1 Corinthians 6:9–10 (NIV)

⁹ Do you not know that wrongdoers will not inherit the kingdom of God? Do not be deceived: Neither the sexually immoral nor idolaters nor adulterers nor men who have sex with men

¹⁰ nor thieves nor the greedy nor drunkards nor slanderers nor swindlers will inherit the kingdom of God.

Remember, I am showing you what God's Word says regarding who will not inherit the kingdom of God. I did not say this, but God's Word says it. If any of these two verses offend you, then you will have to take it up with God. These two verses are clear on who is not going to heaven no matter what a person may want to believe. But if (there is that word if again), if they repent, receive Jesus into their heart, turn away from these sinful things, and obey God's Word before they die, then, and only then, will they go to heaven. The key word here is if.

"Mike, I was born a homosexual," or "Mike, I was born a lesbian," or "I was born a drunk," I say no, you were not born a homosexual, a lesbian, or a drunk. That is the same as saying (examples), I was born a sex offender, I was born an idol worshipper, I was born a killer, I was born a prostitute, I was born an adulterer, I was born a fornicator (fornication: two people having sex when they are not married to each other), I was born a thief, I was born a liar. All of those things are sins against God. Even though we are born sinners, we are not born to be a particular type of sin. The person we become depends on what we choose to allow ourselves to be influenced by.

Note: Unfortunately, there are people who are forced to live the lifestyle that they live. This still does not mean we were born to be what we are today.

Everything that we are taught and everything that happens to us as we are growing up will influence us to be one thing or another or to live one lifestyle or another. We are never just born that way as a baby. I was not born a Christian at birth from my mom. It was all the things that I learned and the things that I experienced in my life that influenced me to become a Christian. Before I became a Christian, I was a drunkard. I was not born a drunk, but I became one. I did not walk around when I was two or three years old with a bottle of alcohol in my hand, saying I was born this way. No one is born to commit a particular sin, but they are influenced into whatever lifestyle they live.

When it comes to sin, no matter what you are today, you were not just born that way. When it comes to sin, as a baby, you had no idea of what you were going to become. If you are not born again, it is your choice if you want to be a Christian or not. It is up to you. You can change; I did. Unfortunately, there are religions and people that teach the wrong ways of how to be saved.

Revelation 20:10–15 (NIV)

[10] And the devil, who deceived them, was thrown into the lake of burning sulfur, where the beast and

the false prophet had been thrown. They will be tormented day and night for ever and ever.

¹¹Then I saw a great white throne and him who was seated on it. The earth and the heavens fled from his presence, and there was no place for them.

¹² And I saw the dead, great and small, standing before the throne, and books were opened. Another book was opened, which is the book of life. The dead were judged according to what they had done as recorded in the books.

¹³The sea gave up the dead that were in it, and death and Hades gave up the dead that were in them, and each person was judged according to what he had done.

¹⁴Then death and Hades were thrown into the lake of fire. The lake of fire is the second death.

¹⁵ Anyone whose name was not found written in the book of life was thrown into the lake of fire.

These verses show things that are to come and what will happen after God brings the world to an end.

In verse 10, it says, the devil who deceived the people. Who did he deceive? All of those who do not believe God's Word. Those who were deceived in one way or another to not believe the Bible. Those who chose to believe their own way instead of the Bible. The devil will be thrown into the lake of burning sulfur, where the beast and the false prophet had been thrown, and "they will be tormented day and night for ever and ever." The torment will last forever.

In verse 11, John saw Jesus Christ sitting on a great white throne; the earth and the heavens fled from Jesus' presence. They found no place to hide.

In verse 12, the books that were opened had everything that each and every person ever said and done written in them. The spiritually dead, the great and the small, no matter who they are, will be judged according to their deeds that are written in the books. And the book of life was opened, and the names of those who are spiritually dead are not written in the book of life.

In verse 13, the sea and death and Hades all gave up the dead to be judged. Every single person will be judged according to what he or she has done.

In verse 14, death and Hades were thrown into the lake of fire, which is the second death. "Why is the lake of fire a second death?" I am glad you asked that question. When a person who has not accepted Jesus as their Savior dies, that is their first death. Their death is a total and complete separation from God. The second death occurs when those who are dead are judged and then thrown into the lake of fire, where they will spend eternity separated from God. They will be tormented forever and ever.

In verse 15, when the body dies, and the person did not accept Jesus as their Savior, then the person's name will not be found in the book of life. Therefore, that person will be thrown into the lake of fire. "Whoever's name is not found in the book of life will be thrown into the lake of fire." If you have received Jesus Christ as your personal Savior, then your name is written in the book of life.

I am not trying to scare you. I am just stating what the Bible says in hopes that you know why it is so important to be born again.

>Revelation 21:7–8 (NIV)
>
>⁷Those who are victorious will inherit all this, and I will be their God and they will be my children.
>
>⁸ But the cowardly, the unbelieving, the vile, the murderers, the sexually immoral, those who practice magic arts, the idolaters and all liars—they will be consigned to the fiery lake of burning sulfur. This is the second death.

If you open your Bible and read Revelation 21:1–6, you will find out what inheritance God is talking about in verse seven. In verse eight, God was making it very clear who is going to hell via the lake of fire.

>As I have said earlier, when we read from
>1 Corinthians 6:9–10 (KJV),
>
>⁹ Know ye not that the unrighteous shall not inherit the kingdom of God? Be not deceived: neither fornicators, nor idolaters, nor adulterers, nor effeminate, nor abusers of themselves with mankind,
>
>¹⁰ Nor thieves, nor covetous, nor drunkards, nor revilers, nor extortioners, shall inherit the kingdom of God.

There is still hope for those who are disobedient if they repent and turn to God before they die. Jesus Christ died and rose again from the dead for the whole world, for all of mankind, the living, the dead in the grave, and for those who were not and are not yet born.

Think about it according to God's Word, not mine, but God's Word. All who do not repent and accept Jesus as their personal Savior will go to the lake of fire and be tormented day and night forever and ever. They will always feel tired, always be in a lot of scrutinizing pain feeling the fire burning on them. They will experience the horrors of pain beyond the imagination. This is what Jesus Christ has saved us from.

When God is talking about the new heaven and earth in Revelation 21:1-6, God had John write in verse four that God will wipe away every tear from our eyes and that there will be no more pain or death or mourning or crying for these things have passed away. There will be a new heaven and a new earth.

Revelation 21:4 (NIV)

> ⁴ He will wipe every tear from their eyes. There will be no more death or mourning or crying or pain, for the old order of things has passed away.

What a total difference between going to hell and going to heaven. In hell, one will suffer forever. Heaven is just the opposite of hell. Those who have received Christ will go to heaven and never again experience anguish, sorrow, mourning, or grief. They will never see death nor have pain again. They will never experience anything bad again.

The sad part is that not everyone is going to heaven. I am pleading with you: if you are not one already, to be one of the few who are going to heaven. Do not wait until it is too late and you hear it being said that your name is not in the book of life, and Jesus says, "Depart from Me, for I do not know you." If you have not accepted Jesus Christ already as your personal Savior, then accept Him now. Pray the prayer of salvation that is written at the end of chapter 6, and then be a doer of the Word.

Jesus saved us from hell. God does not want anyone to go there. That is why God gave us Jesus Christ, His Son. God gave us the Bible so we know what to believe and what not to believe. The Bible shows us how to stay on the straight and narrow road to heaven by being a doer of the Word and not by being a doer of man-made beliefs. Man-made beliefs can lead you away from God and get you to believe wrong things about Him. Read your Bible, and quit deceiving, betraying, and fooling yourself.

I was asked what my interpretation is of why the gate to heaven is narrow and the gate to hell is wide. I have no scriptural answer other than Jesus said it. Let's try to look at it in a biblical way, and in a practical sense. It is hard for a lot of people to go through a narrow gate when they do not choose the right way to go through it. A lot of people choose to believe and practice the wrong ways to get into heaven. Therefore, the gate to heaven is narrow. It is easier for a lot of people to go through a wide gate than it is to go through a narrow gate. It is easier for people to continually believe and practice the wrong ways, believing that by their way, they are still going to heaven. Why? Because people are stubborn, they still want to believe their beliefs are right even though the Bible says their beliefs are wrong. Many people believe and practice the wrong things to get into heaven. They try and fail. Therefore, the gate to hell is wide because many are going there.

There is another way to look at what Jesus meant. People will find it easier to live a sinful life than it is to live a life without sin. It is easier to go through a wide gate than it is to go through a narrow gate. Therefore, the gate to hell is wide, and the gate to heaven is narrow.

Unfortunately, there are a lot of people that are set in their ways and beliefs. People think different strokes for different folks, what works for you is not for me. Sin is not always doing something bad to someone. There are a lot of sins that are fun, exciting, and even gratifying. The lust of the eyes, the lust of the flesh, the pride of life, and the deceitfulness of riches, thinking the riches will solve their problems. People want what they want and do not realize these sins are enslaving them, separating them from God, and sending them to hell.

Side note: Being rich is not a sin. Praying to God for finances to meet your needs is not a sin. It is the love of money, greed, and lust for it that is a sin. It is the use of money to control or manipulate others that is a sin. Having money is not a sin. It is what you do with it or how you feel about it if it becomes sin or not.

Too many people say, "I go to church on Sundays. I know God. I know Jesus." They think they are going to heaven because they go to church and know about God and Jesus. Going to church and knowing about God and Jesus does not mean they are going to heaven and that they have a personal relationship with God and Jesus. To say I know God and Jesus is the same as saying I know Ben Franklin, Abraham Lincoln, and Mark Twain. We know of them and about them, but we do not know them personally.

People can know about God and Jesus but not know them personally. People who know God and Jesus personally no longer have a desire to live sinful lives. They desire to read the Bible and be a doer of the Word, living for Christ. Too many people do not know God and Jesus personally and have not taken the gift of God, His Son, Jesus Christ, as their personal Lord and Savior. This is why the gate to hell is wide.

If people do not have a strong desire to repent, to get rid of all the sinful things in their lives, or want to live a life without sin, then they do not know God and Jesus. They only know about Them.

Jesus did His part to save us; now, He wants us to do our part to choose Him and go to heaven. What did Jesus save us from? He saved us from sin, spiritual death, and going to hell!

CHAPTER 14:

BEING A DOER OF THE WORD AND BEING HOLY

God wants us to be a doer of the Word and to be holy.

James 1:22–25 (NIV)

²² Do not merely listen to the word, and so deceive yourselves. Do what it says.

²³ Anyone who listens to the word but does not do what it says is like someone who looks at his face in a mirror

²⁴ and, after looking at himself, goes away and immediately forgets what he looks like.

²⁵ But whoever looks intently into the perfect law that gives freedom, and continues in it—not forgetting what he has heard, but doing it—they will be blessed in what they do.

Verses 22 and 23 are saying if you are just a listener and not a doer of the Word, you are deceiving, betraying, and fooling yourself. Reading your Bible and going to church is part of being a doer of God's Word. God does not want you to just listen to or merely hear the Word but rather to be a doer of the Word. Attend a Bible-believing church. God wants you to go to church to be taught the Word, to fellowship, and to be supported by other like-minded believers. Going to church will help you grow in understanding the Bible. God also wants you to go to church to worship Him with others.

"Okay, Mike. I've got it. We are to be doers of the Word. But just what does that mean?" I am glad you asked that question. To be a doer of the Word means to put into "practice" or "act" on the Word.

"Okay, now I got to ask, how do I put into practice or act on the Word?" To practice and act on the Word means to apply it to every aspect of your life by doing what God teaches us to do in His Word. You will not be a doer of everything in the Bible overnight. It takes time. But you can start to act on and/or practice what you learn from the Bible as you read it.

Do not be like the person who goes to see his doctor because he is dying, and after listening to his doctor on how to stay alive, he goes his way and does not follow his doctor's orders and, therefore, dies. Reading the Bible and then not doing what it says is the same thing. Being a doer of the Word helps us to win the spiritual battle of death.

Our goal as a doer of the Word is to become more like Christ in our everyday life. We need to line up our thoughts with the Word. When we do that, our actions will follow. Being a doer of the Word does not make you holier than thou...but it does make you obedient to the Word of God. The more you practice and act on what the Word teaches, the more you become like Christ, and that is pleasing to God the Father. Does anyone ever become exactly like Jesus Christ? No. Does anyone do every command that is in the Bible? No. We can only do the best that we can to be a doer of the Word.

God says to be a doer of the Word. The Bible is the Word. Do we always obey the Word? No! Because we are human, and none of us can become perfect. If we did, God would not have put verses in the Bible like the following.

Jesus is speaking in Matthew 7:21, 24; Luke 6:46.

Matthew 7:21 (KJV)

[21] "Not every one that saith unto me, Lord, Lord, shall enter into the kingdom of heaven; but he that doeth the will of my Father which is in heaven."

Matthew 7:24 (NIV)

[24] "Therefore everyone who hears these words of mine and puts them into practice is like a wise man who built his house on the rock."

Luke 6:46 (KJV)

[46] "And why call ye me, Lord, Lord, and do not the things which I say?" (Ouch!)

James 1:22 (KJV)

[22] "But be ye doers of the word, and not hearers only, deceiving your own selves."

These four verses speak for themselves. They point out some of the importance of being a doer of the Word.

Acting on the Word means to accept the whole Bible as the written Word of God. God will never give us the authority to choose or pick what to believe or what not to believe in the Bible. God did not inspire man to write the Bible for a later time period, leaving it for us to pick what we should or should not believe. God wants us to believe the whole Bible and never wants it changed because of how we live or to change it as the world dictates. The books of the Bible, or the books that are in the Bible, are the only books that God wants us to accept as the true written Word of God. These books are the only ones that met all of the canonizing requirements to prove that they are inspired by God.

The Holy Spirit gives us the desire to be a doer of the Word. The Holy Spirit shows and reveals things to us as we read the Bible. The scriptures in the Bible will come alive to us because God will talk to us through the Holy Spirit as we read the Bible. I do not know how to explain it, but you will know when the Holy Spirit is showing you something in the Bible that will help you out in life or will help you to understand something.

I am sure there are others who feel like I did when I became born again and was told that I needed to be a doer of the Word. Yes, I had a fear of not knowing what it would be like to live this way. I found out we still live a normal life. The biggest change in our lives is getting to know God and learning how to live a life without sin. Contrary to the world's popular belief, we can have a personal relationship with God, Jesus Christ, and the Holy Spirit. We can live without sin. This is possible for everyone who is born again. Still, this does not mean you will never sin again.

When a person becomes born again and does not become a doer of the Word, that person is making it hard for themself to be obedient to God. In effect, the person is telling God that he/she does not love Him. Again, in John 14:15, Jesus said, "If you love Me, keep My commands." He was only talking about the commands that are in the Bible. He was not talking about religious commands that people come up with that are not in the Bible.

Satan will do everything he can to get us to not be doers of the Word. But God has given us victory over him through Jesus Christ (1 Corinthians 15:57). By applying the Word to our everyday lives, we can win spiritual battles.

A side note for those who don't know: once we become born again, God does not want us to continue practicing religious beliefs that are not in the Bible or do not line up with the Bible. I have come across people who did not know this.

Not only does God want us to be a doer of the Word but He wants us to be holy.

> 1 Peter 1:15–16 (KJV)
>
> [15] But as he which hath called you is holy, so be ye holy in all manner of conversation; [16] because it is written, "Be holy, for I am holy."

Be holy, for God is holy. Being holy is not acting holier than thou. Being holy is a way of life and is not being all puffed up thinking you're better than someone else. "Mike, why do you keep coming up with acting holier than thou?" Because I have come across too many people with the idea that this is what being holy is and what a doer of the Word means. When a Christian says we need to live a life without sin and to be holy, the nonbeliever's first thought or concept is that this person thinks they're better than everyone else. This is not true.

Being holy is simply having a relationship with God, and we do this by reading and acting on His Word. It is striving to be like Jesus, treating others with respect and not looking down at others as if they are lower than us. It is being obedient to God through His Word. This is being a doer of the Word and being holy.

According to the Bible, we cannot be holy if we are not doers of the Word and are still living a life of sin.

This simply means we need:

1. To act on and practice what the Scriptures are teaching us by doing what the Word says.

2. To change our lives by turning away from sin and lining up our lives with the commands in the Bible to the best of our ability.

3. To change and stop our sinful behavior and our sinful ways of thinking by getting rid of them and not yielding our mind and body to temptation.

To be good at anything in life one has to read and study all about whatever they want to be good at. Then, they have to put into practice what they have learned. It is the same with being a doer of the Word. The key to being a doer of the Word is studying and reading the Bible, putting into practice God's commands that are in the Bible. When we obey God's commands, we show God that we love Him. Once we become born again the Holy Spirit comes and dwells in us. He helps us and gives us the desire to be a doer of the Word.

Being holy is a part of being a doer of the Word. I want to say one more thing about being holy. Look at what God says in the Bible about born-again believers.

Exodus 19:5–6 (KJV)

⁵ Now therefore, if ye will obey my voice indeed, and keep my covenant, then ye shall be a peculiar treasure unto me above all people: for all the earth is mine:

⁶ And ye shall be unto me a kingdom of priests, and an holy nation. These are the words which thou shalt speak unto the children of Israel.

Because the Jewish leaders of the children of Israel rejected Jesus when He was alive here on Earth, God made this prophecy to be true even for the Gentiles (Gentiles, that's us).

1 Peter 2:9 (KJV)

⁹ But ye are a chosen generation, a royal priesthood, an holy nation, a peculiar people; that ye should shew forth the praises of him who hath called you out of darkness into his marvellous light.

Man, the world, the unbeliever has the wrong ideas of what being holy is all about. In 1 Peter 1:16, Peter was quoting Leviticus 11:44. He was not just addressing spiritual leaders but he was addressing every single average common believer. Those verses address everyone, both you and me. God wants everyone, every believer, to be holy, for He is holy.

Religious leaders are not the only ones that can be holy. Practicing and performing religious ceremonies does not make a person holy. People can be as religious as they want and still not be holy because being religious does not make one holy. When a person acts like or believes he/she is holier than thou, that person is not being holy. In Exodus 19:5–6, God is talking about anyone who is obedient to Him. In 1 Peter 2:9, Peter is saying this to all believers, quoting Exodus 19:5–6, saying this is about all believers.

Again, contrary to the world's popular belief, we are a chosen generation, a royal priesthood, an holy nation, and a peculiar people because we are doers of the Word. You do not have to be a church leader, a pastor or priest, a bishop, or the Pope in order to be holy! If—If you are born again, a doer of the Word striving to the best of your ability to live a life for Christ, and you have a personal relationship with Jesus Christ and God, then you are holy. Being holy is being a doer of the Word because when you are a doer of the Word, that is what makes you Holy.

I must add that there are acts of ritual commands in the Old Testament (the old convent) that no longer need to be practiced and that have been done away with by the new convent (the New Testament) through the blood and resurrection of Jesus Christ. Plus, there are religious beliefs that God does not want us to practice or believe because they are not in the Bible and/or they are taken out of context from the Bible. That is why I say so often to read your Bible.

CHAPTER 15:

JESUS IS OUR ADVOCATE AND MEDIATOR

Knowing who to pray to and why and who not to pray to is a part of being born again. Knowing what Jesus Christ is to us is basic to being born again. Here are some of the things that Jesus is to us.

The Bible tells us that Jesus is the only human advocate and mediator that man has with God. An advocate is someone who pleads your case for a wrongdoing or wrongdoings. In our case, Jesus pleads to God, the Father, for the forgiveness of our sins. A mediator is someone who communicates between two people, to work things out. In our case, it is to bring us, you and I, back to God. This is why we go to Jesus, because He is the one and only one who can get our sins forgiven and make us right with God. This is because Jesus is the only one who died to save us.

1 Timothy 2:5-6 (NIV).

⁵ For there is one God and one mediator between God and mankind, the man Christ Jesus, ⁶ who gave himself as a ransom for all people. This has now been witnessed to at the proper time.

Chapter 15: Jesus Is Our Advocate and Mediator

1 John 2:1-2 (NIV)

¹ My dear children, I write this to you so that you will not sin. But if anybody does sin, we have an advocate with the Father—Jesus Christ, the Righteous One.

² He is the atoning sacrifice for our sins, and not only for ours but also for the sins of the whole world.

One of the reasons why God had Timothy start out with "there is one God and one mediator between God and men, the man Christ Jesus." The Amplified Bible brings out the reason. There is only one God, only one mediator: the man Christ Jesus, because Jesus is the only mediator! The key words are "there is only one." In 1 John, Jesus is the only human named as the advocate because He is the only one who died to save us. No other human can be an advocate or a mediator between God and man or between Jesus and man because no other human died to give us our salvation. Christ Jesus is the only advocate and the only mediator between God and man, and there is none given to us between Jesus and man. There is no one else. No one!

Part of the point that Timothy is bringing out here is that just as there is only one God, there is only one mediator. There are no other mediators. Besides Jesus Christ, there are no other mediators between God and man, and there are none between man and Jesus Christ.

First John 2:1 says that if we do sin, we have an advocate; an advocate is one who pleads the case of another. Jesus intercedes for us with God, and just like God the Father, Jesus can and does pardon (forgive) us of our sins. The Jews understood that only God has the authority to pardon sin, and this is one of the reasons why they wanted Jesus dead because He told a man his sins were forgiven. The Jews did not believe that Jesus was God, so they felt, "How dare Jesus forgive someone of their sins?" In 1 John chapter 2, John is talking about when a Christian sins because Christians do sin. When a Christian commits a sin and repents, Jesus pardons him/her of their sin. He regains God's favor for them and brings them back to God. Look at the what and how of what is being said in 1 John. John is talking about the sins that Christians commit after they are saved, not of the sins committed before they were saved. Jesus is our advocate, our mediator; He intercedes for us when we sin. Jesus not only died to make atonement for our sin He now sits at the right hand of God as our intercessor.

> Hebrews 10:12 (ESV)
>
> [12] But when Christ had offered for all time a single sacrifice for sins, he sat down at the right hand of God.
>
> Romans 8:34 (ESV)
>
> [34] Who is to condemn? Christ Jesus is the one who died—more than that, who was raised—who is at the right hand of God, who indeed is interceding for us.

Besides Jesus dwelling in us, He is seated at the right hand of God, interceding for us.

God said in the Bible that there is only one mediator, and He is our advocate; this is Christ Jesus. Nowhere in the New Testament does God say that someone else is to be a mediator or an advocate between God and men; Jesus is the only one. Nor does God say that there is to be an advocate or a mediator between

Jesus and man. The Bible says that Jesus Christ is our advocate and mediator. If God wanted us to go to someone else to get to Jesus, to ask Jesus to go to God for our sins, He would have told us so in the Bible, and He did not. Jesus Christ is our advocate. Jesus Christ is our mediator. Jesus Christ is our propitiation, the atoning sacrifice of our sins. That is why we are to ask only Jesus and God for the forgiveness of our sins.

Before Jesus died on the cross for our sins, according to the Scriptures (the Old Testament), a live, unblemished animal or animals had to be brought to the high priest as a sacrifice for one's sin. The high priest had to then kill the animals and shed their blood on the altar. That was the only way a person could get their sins forgiven.

The moment Jesus Christ died on the cross, He once and for all became the ultimate sacrifice. No more sacrifices have to be made. Whenever an animal was sacrificed on the altar for one's sin, it only got the sins forgiven, but people still did not have a way to enter heaven. When Jesus died and rose from the dead, and went to heaven, He changed all of that.

"Why is Jesus Christ the ultimate sacrifice?" One, because there are no more sacrifices needed to be made for our sins. Two, because everybody's sin (in the whole world, past, present, and future) was on Jesus Christ when He died on the cross. Three, Jesus took our punishment for our sins. He paid the price and shed His blood for our sins. That is why Jesus Christ is the ultimate sacrifice. When we receive Jesus as our personal Lord and Savior, not only are we forgiven, but we are going to heaven. I know a lot of you know these three reasons by now, but I needed to make it very clear that God does not want us to go to anyone but Jesus to get our sins forgiven.

Nowhere in the New Testament does it say that there is a mediator or advocate between Jesus and man. Look again at what we just read in 1 Timothy 2:5-6, 1 John 2:1-2, and 1 John 4:10. See for yourself that these verses do not say that anyone else is a mediator or an advocate between God and man or between Jesus and man. These verses say that Jesus is the only one. Why? Because Jesus *is* the only one who died and paid the penalty for our sins.

James 5:16 (KJV)

¹⁶ Confess your faults one to another, and pray one for another, that ye may be healed. The effectual fervent prayer of a righteous man availeth much.

Psalm 32:5 (ESV)

⁵ I acknowledged my sin to you, and I did not cover my iniquity; I said, "I will confess my transgressions to the LORD," and you forgave the iniquity of my sin. Selah.

First John 1:9 (KJV)

⁹ If we confess our sins, he is faithful and just to forgive us our sins, and to cleanse us from all unrighteousness."

James 5:16 says to confess your sins to one another and pray for one another, that you may be healed. It does not say, "Confess your sins to one another and pray for one another so that you can go to God to ask Him to forgive someone else for their sins." Psalm 32:51 and 1 John 1:9 say that when we confess our sins to the Lord, He is faithful and just to forgive us our sins. When we confess our own sins to God, He is the one who is faithful and just to forgive us our sins and to cleanse us from all unrighteousness. There is only one mediator and advocate between God and man for the forgiveness of sin, and that is Jesus Christ.

I was told Jesus intercedes for us. This is true, but if Jesus does not plead our case to God the Father for us, then let us change the definition of the word advocate, which means one who pleads the cause for others. Cause—a suit or an action in court: case. First John 2:1 talks about when a person sins and that Jesus is our advocate. You will find the word advocate in most English translations of the Bible. Did the scholars who know how to read and translate Greek into English use the wrong word and get it wrong? I don't think so. If Jesus does not plead to God the Father for the forgiveness of our sins, then let us not call Him our advocate. Jesus Christ is my advocate (one who pleads), and He pleads to God the Father for the forgiveness of my sins. Having said all of that, and that God and Jesus are a forgiving God, we still should not take the verses about repenting lightly.

God does not want us to ask a religion, a man, a woman, or anyone else for the forgiveness of our sins. Yes, you are to ask for forgiveness from someone when you do something wrong to them, but not for them to go to Jesus for the forgiveness of your sin. Nowhere in the New Testament does it say for us to ask someone else to go to Jesus for the forgiveness of our sins.

Note: A clarification of one of the reasons why Jesus Christ was crucified. In the Old Testament, under the old covenant, a person had to have the high priest sacrifice an animal or animals to get their sins forgiven. In the New Testament, under the new covenant, Jesus Christ was sacrificed to get everyone's sins forgiven. Today, Jesus Christ is the only high priest. Jesus Christ is the only one that we can go to to receive God's forgiveness of our sins. Why? Because Jesus Christ is the only one who was sacrificed for the forgiveness of our sins. No one else can go to God for us for the forgiveness of our sins because they were not sacrificed for our sins. My point is Jesus Christ is the only one we can go to in order to get God's forgiveness of our sins.

No matter how many times you sin, fail, or fall flat on your face, you can ask for forgiveness, and Jesus will plead to God the Father for forgiveness, and He will forgive you. (Note: Jesus pleading for our sins, not doctrinal? Advocate—meaning one who pleads for others. Again, read 1 John 2:1–2. Did your parents, after a certain number of times of disobedience, stop forgiving you? No! Does God say in the New Testament, "Oops, you sinned one too many times, and you're a Christian now; I cannot forgive you anymore?" No!) But God still wants us to live a life without sin. Remember, sin kills our spirit by separating us from God.

Having said how forgiving God is, that does not mean it is okay for us to sin whenever because we know God will forgive us. Yes, God will forgive us, but it does not make it right or okay for us to sin. We still need to strive to live a life without sin because sin does separate us from God.

God points out to us in the Bible that there is only one mediator, who is our advocate, and He is Jesus Christ, the righteous one. We are given no one else other than Jesus Christ. He is the only one given to us as a mediator and an advocate in the Bible. Anything that you need prayer for, you can pray to God, the three-in-one, through Jesus Christ, our mediator.

John 14:13 (KJV)

¹³ And whatsoever ye shall ask in my name, that will I do, that the Father may be glorified in the Son.

The same is said in John 15:16; 16:23, 26. Jesus said, whatever you ask for, ask in His name so the Father may be glorified in the Son. Whatever we ask for, we are to ask for it in the name of Jesus. Jesus is the only mediator.

God does not want to have a third-party relationship; He wants a one-on-one relationship with you.

Deuteronomy 18:10–12 (ESV)

¹⁰ There shall not be found among you anyone who burns his son or his daughter as an offering, anyone who practices divination or tells fortunes or interprets omens, or a sorcerer

¹¹ or a charmer or a medium or a necromancer or one who inquires of the dead,

¹² for whoever does these things is an abomination to the LORD. And because of these abominations the LORD your God is driving them out before you.

God does not approve of a consulter with familiar spirits, or anyone who practices divination, or tells fortunes, or interprets omens, or a sorcerer, or a medium, or one who inquires of the dead, or a necromancer. Necromancer means the practice of talking to the spirits of the dead, or people who summon the dead to fight for them, or masters of the dark arts.

You will be told by some people, "Well, I don't talk to the dead because they are alive in heaven." You can tell them this: It does not matter if they are dead in hell or alive in heaven; when the Bible talks about people being dead, their physical body is dead. According to God and His Bible, dead means anyone who lived and died and went to hell or heaven; they are *dead*. If they are not alive in a physical body here on Earth, they are dead. The only person this does not apply to is Jesus because He is God.

No one on Earth or in heaven can become omnipresent like God. No one can be on Earth and in heaven at the same time. This would make them equal to God. God will not make anyone or allow anyone to be equal to Him. Once they are in heaven, they cannot come back to Earth unless Jesus brings them back to life. No saint in heaven has the power to answer prayer. Again, this would make them equal to God.

If you are born again, Jesus and the Holy Spirit are dwelling in your body with you. They are always with you. Why have a mediator to talk to Jesus when He is right there with you? What an insult that must be to Jesus. Again, Jesus is the only mediator. There are no other mediators between God and man nor between Jesus and man. There is no need for a mediator between you and Jesus when He is right there with and in you. Praying and talking to God and Jesus through someone else is the same as talking to anyone you know standing next to you through a third person. What an insult!

When you pray to God do not just ask for things, but remember to thank Him for things. Talk to God, Jesus Christ, and the Holy Spirit. They are the same one God, and at the same time, they are three separate individuals wanting to have a personal relationship with you. Pray and talk to them on a daily basis; this is a part of being born again.

CHAPTER 16:

DID JESUS HAVE BROTHERS AND SISTERS?

"Did Jesus have brothers and sisters?" Well, first, we have to ask, did Mary stay a virgin her whole life? What does the Bible say?

Scholars translate the Bible into English so we can read and understand the Bible. Then, we are told by some religions that the translations of some verses are not what the Bible is saying. This seems to happen whenever someone is trying to prove a belief that they want us to believe when it is not doctrinally stated in the Bible.

Note: I will not name the commentaries I am talking about in order to not be publicly slandering them. This belief is one of the few beliefs that I disagree on with them. This belief is one of where one would say you can't believe everything in the Bible because it is, I quote, "written by man." *But* you can or are supposed to believe what is not in the Bible that is "written by man." Let us look at the stated facts in the Bible and the theories that are written by man that say the stated facts in the Bible are wrong to prove their beliefs are right. We need to think through what is being said in the Bible and why it is being said. We need to look at how ridiculous the theories are. Man's written stated theories versus the Bible-stated facts.

Chapter 16: Did Jesus Have Brothers and Sisters?

Matthew 1:23–25 (NIV)

²³ "The virgin will conceive and give birth to a son, and they will call him Immanuel" (which means "God with us").

²⁴ When Joseph woke up, he did what the angel of the Lord had commanded him and took Mary home as his wife.

²⁵ But he did not consummate their marriage until she gave birth to a son. And he gave him the name Jesus.

I read at least eleven commentaries on Matthew 1:25. They all focused on the word "till" in the verse. They say the word "till" is being used differently as to what it means. One commentary refers us to Psalm 110:1 (KJV), "1 The LORD said unto my Lord, Sit thou at my right hand, until I made thine enemies thy footstool." God is talking to Jesus in this verse. The commentary says this is how "until" is being used in both verses. Quote, "Until is being a particle only exclusive of a preceding time, not affirming the thing in future time." This is implying the word until or till is not talking of a future event occurring after a past event has happened. This is like saying the words "was" and "is" in certain sentences do not necessarily imply past and present tense. Think about it. This is indirectly saying the word "till" is not being used properly in Matthew 1:25. Because of the wording in Psalm 110:1, "until" is being used the way the commentary says it is. However, there is no proof or evidence that "until" is being used that same way in Matthew 1:25. We have to remember Psalm 110:1 was written in Hebrew, and Matthew 1:25 was written in Greek. They are comparing a word from two different languages on what it means when translated into English. It is only a false theory to deny what Matthew 1:25 is saying, that Mary did not stay a virgin. This verse is to prove that she was a virgin when she gave birth to Jesus Christ.

Looking at Psalm 110:1, God is talking about spiritual events happening in *His* sense of time, not *physical*, earthly events happening in *our sense of time*, like in Matthew 1:25. When using the word till or until, we cannot compare God's reality of time with ours. Why? Because they are not the same. Second Peter 3:8 (KJV) says, "8 But, beloved, be not ignorant of this one thing, that one day is with the Lord as a thousand years, and a thousand years as one day." God's reality of time is not past, present, and future, or until, was, and is; ours is, but God's time is always now.

Then, they focus on verses about Jesus being Mary's firstborn. Therefore, they say, "In conclusion, this does not necessarily imply that she had other children, though it seems probable." Remember, according to some people, even though the Bible was inspired by God, we are not supposed to believe everything in the Bible because it was "written by man." But we are supposed to believe everything that was "written by man" that is not in the Bible and was not inspired by God. They want us to believe things that are not in agreement with the Bible, that are "written by man."

Another commentary says, "A historical article of Joseph makes him to be a worn-out old man. Joseph most likely did not have sexual intercourse with Mary." This same man, who was too old and worn out to have sex, was able to travel long distances with Mary, according to the Gospels. He could not have been too old and worn out to have sex if he had the strength to travel long distances. Joseph walked while Mary rode a donkey. I read Matthew 1:25 in twenty-five different English translations. Even though they are worded a little differently, they all state the same thing. Joseph and Mary had sex after Mary gave birth to Jesus. Let's examine the sentence structure of how the verse is worded in the English language.

In the King James English, when a man "knew" a woman, it meant they had sex. Consummate means the marriage was made complete by having sexual intercourse. "Joseph knew her not, did not consummate their marriage 'until' meaning after Jesus was born." In the commentaries, they say this does not necessarily imply that they had sexual intercourse. That's funny. Till or until always means something did not happen until after something else has happened. This means that, eventually, it did happen. Yet, those who wrote the commentaries I read say this does not necessarily imply that they had sexual intercourse after Jesus was born. Remember, consummate means a married couple did have sex. King James or 1600s English, if a couple knew each other, they had sex.

Examples: The water did not stop coming out of the faucet until it was turned off. Now, even though we are told that the water stopped coming out, the commentaries say, "Oh, this does not necessarily imply that the water stopped coming out when the faucet was turned off." The rock did not stop falling until it hit the bottom of the pit. Now, even though we are told that the rock stopped falling when it hit the bottom of the pit, the commentaries say, "Oh, this does not necessarily imply that the rock stopped falling when it hit the bottom of the pit. It may have fallen another fifty feet after it hit the bottom of the pit." Even though it says until, the commentaries say, "This does not necessarily imply that Joseph did consummate their marriage after Jesus was born." Really? My point is, how can anyone say Joseph did not consummate their marriage when Scripture says, "He did not consummate their marriage *until* she gave birth to a son"?

Matthew was inspired by God to write that Mary and Joseph did not consummate their marriage until after Jesus was born. Therefore, Mary was a virgin until after Jesus was born. This statement is evidence to further prove that Mary was a virgin when she gave birth to Jesus. But she did not stay a virgin after Jesus was born. Face it, the verse is saying they had sex after Jesus was born.

Matthew 1:25 is not implying that Joseph and Mary may have had sex after Jesus was born; it states they did have sex after Jesus was born.

Mark 6:1–3 (ESV)

¹ He went away from there and came to his hometown, and his disciples followed him.

² And on the Sabbath he began to teach in the synagogue, and many who heard him were astonished, saying, "Where did this man get these things? What is the wisdom given to him? How are such mighty works done by his hands?

³ Is not this the carpenter, the son of Mary and brother of James and Joses and Judas and Simon? And are not his sisters here with us?" And they took offense at him.

Matthew 13:54–56 says the same thing about what happened here in these verses. Jesus was a carpenter all His life before He started His ministry. These verses do not say what Jesus taught, but they do say the people were astonished. They were so astonished by His great wisdom and the mighty works done by His hands that this offended them. This is Jesus' hometown and home synagogue, where everyone had known Him for a long time and watched Him grow up. In all the years that they knew Him they never heard such wisdom come out of Him. Now, all of a sudden, He has great wisdom and has done mighty works. How can this be? Where did He get this ability?

They just could not understand how a man who had done carpentry work all His life could have so much wisdom about God and perform mighty miracles. To them, He was just a carpenter. In disbelief, they immediately chose to discredit Jesus by pointing out how well they knew Him. They were saying, "Look, we know who He is; we can't believe Him." "Is not this the carpenter, the son of Mary, the brother of James, Joseph, Juda, and Simon? And are not his sisters here with us?" They knew who Jesus' blood relatives were.

Jesus had four half-brothers, James, Joseph, Judas, and Simon, and some half-sisters who lived among the people. Half-brothers and half-sisters because they were born of Mary and Joseph, not of Mary and the Holy Spirit. No, the Holy Spirit and Mary did not have sex. The Holy Spirit just put the seed of Jesus' body in her.

It is said that the half-brothers and sisters are not Jesus' brothers and sisters, but they are His cousins or brothers and sisters in Christ. I have to ask some "why" and "if" questions on this. If they are not Jesus' brothers and sisters but His cousins, then why did they say the brother of and His sisters? Again, this was Jesus' hometown and home synagogue; all the people knew who Jesus' relatives were. They did not have to lie to each other. Why didn't they just say His cousins? Why didn't God have Matthew and Mark say, "But the people knew that they really were not Jesus' brothers and sisters"? Lineage was and is very important to the Jews, and it is important to them to be correct on the lineage of everyone. These were Jews pointing out who His relatives were.

Why ask something wrong when everyone there already knew the answers? They were not asking these questions because they did not know the answers but because they wanted to discredit what Jesus was saying by showing that they knew Him and His relatives.

They were asking the answers. They knew He was a carpenter. They knew Mary was His mother. They knew His blood brothers. They knew His blood sisters. They asked the answers because they knew the answers. Let's look at more proof.

Why did they say in verse 3 the words "the brother of" and "His sisters" if these were His cousins? They meant Jesus' blood brothers and sisters. If they were wrong or lying, why didn't God do like He always does when someone is wrong and point out these were His cousins? Why didn't God have Matthew and Mark point out that Jesus did not have any brothers and sisters? If the brothers and sisters in this verse were not Jesus' brothers and sisters, God would have mentioned it in the following verses of what they said, and He did not. The Greek word *adelphos* in Mark 6:3 means brother, not cousin. The Greek word brother being used here means one who is born from the same parent or parents, from the same father and mother. In Jesus' case, it is the same mother. If these four men were Jesus' cousins, then why would the people in Jesus' hometown say "the brother of" instead of "the cousin of"? They knew the lineage of His relatives and their relationship to Jesus. They had no reason for saying the wrong things regarding His relationship to them. They would have been lying to themselves. God is always precise on what is the truth in the Bible. If they were not His brothers and sisters, God would have stated it. If Mary, the mother of Jesus, had stayed a virgin her whole life, God would have stated it in the Bible, and He did not. My point is they knew who Jesus' relatives were, before they asked the questions. They stated the questions correctly. They are His brothers and sisters. There was no benefit to themselves by asking wrong questions. They were simply pointing out Jesus' family because they did not believe what He was teaching them.

To make a certain point, I want to focus on Jesus' half-brother, James, because he is the only one mentioned in Galatians 1:19 (KJV), "But other of the apostles saw I none, save James the Lord's brother." The verse is saying, "I saw none except or only James, the Lord's brother." Using other verses and with the opinion of a person in "Dict. of the Bible," the one commentary said the brother in Galatians 1:19 was Jesus' brother from Joseph's former marriage. I never heard this before, that Joseph was married and had children before he married Mary. There are no stated facts in the Bible saying Joseph had children from a former marriage. The Gospel of Matthew was written to the Jews. Matthew knew how important lineage was to the Jews. If Joseph had a former marriage, Matthew would have mentioned it and said that Jesus had a step-brother or step-brothers.

According to the commentaries I read on Mark 6:3 and Matthew 13:55, James is not a brother but a cousin because His aunt Mary had a son by that name and the theory implies that Jesus cannot have brothers and cousins with the same first names. Then, later on in Galatians 1:19, one of the commentaries says this James is a brother of the Lord from a former marriage of Joseph. "Oops!" Now Jesus can have a brother and cousin with the same first name because this brother is from Joseph's former marriage and not from Joseph and Mary.

One has to think of what is wrong with this picture. The theory is in Mark 6:3 and Matthew 13:55. Jesus *cannot* have a half-brother and a cousin with the same first name, James, because this would mean the half-brother would have been born of Mary and Joseph. Therefore, to prove that Mary stayed a virgin, James is a cousin. But in Galatians 1:19, Jesus *can have* a step-brother and a cousin with the same first name, James, because this brother was born of Joseph's former marriage before Joseph married Mary. Therefore, Jesus can have a step-brother and a cousin with the same first name, James, because this brother was not born of Mary and Joseph.

Note: According to one of the commentaries I read, the thought or theory is, I quote, "Some have been of opinion that a third James," and it goes on and on. The James in Galatians 1:19 might be a third James in the Bible. The verse does not refer to James as a half-brother or a step-brother but only as the Lord's brother. *If* this James is the Lord's brother, a son of Joseph's former wife, then he would be a step-brother to Jesus. This theory is to try to prove that Mary stayed a virgin after Jesus was born.

So! The theory is Jesus *cannot have* half-brothers and cousins with the same first names because this would mean that Mary did not stay a virgin. Therefore, these brothers have to be His cousins, *but* Jesus can have a brother and a cousin with the same first name because this brother is not born of Mary but of Joseph from a former marriage. Therefore, He *can have* a brother and a cousin with the same first name because this is a step-brother not born of Mary. What is wrong with this picture? Again, Mary did not stay a virgin after Jesus was born. Jesus had half-brothers.

The belief that Mary stayed a virgin her whole life is based on theories and opinions; none of it is based on directly stated facts from the Bible.

The Bible does not say that Joseph was married before he married Mary. Whenever the Scriptures mention Jesus' brothers and sisters, the verses do not state any of them as being His cousins or step-brothers from a former marriage of Joseph's. The scriptures simply point out, by how they are worded, that Jesus had brothers and sisters.

Then, there is the stated fact inspired by God in Matthew 1:25 (NIV), "25 But he [Joseph] did not consummate [did not have sex in] their marriage until [after—*after*] she gave birth to a son. And he gave him the name Jesus." Mary did not stay a virgin after Jesus was born. She was not a virgin her whole life, and yes, Jesus had half-brothers and sisters who were born of Mary and Joseph.

CHAPTER 17:

WHEN IS A PICTURE OR STATUE A GRAVEN IMAGE OR IDOL?

"Mike, what is a graven image?" It is a picture or statue of any physical image that people praise, worship, and pray to. God speaks strongly against graven images of any type for worship and commands us not to have them. Deuteronomy chapter 4 confirms and expounds a little more on the second commandment. Here are the first three commandments of the ten commandments in the Bible, in Exodus chapter 20 and Deuteronomy chapter 5.

Exodus 20:3–5 (NLT)

³ You must not have any other god but me.

⁴ You must not make for yourself an idol of any kind or an image of anything in the heavens or on the earth or in the sea.

⁵ You must not bow down to them or worship them, for I, the LORD your God, am a jealous God who will not tolerate your affection for any other gods. I lay the sins of the parents upon their children; the entire family is affected—even children in the third and fourth generation of those who rejected me.

These three commandments are repeated in Deuteronomy 5:7–9, as the rest of the commandments are repeated in Deuteronomy chapter 5.

Deuteronomy 4:16–17 (NLT)

[16] So do not corrupt yourselves by making an idol in any form—whether of a man or a woman, 17 an animal on the ground, a bird in the sky.

Isaiah 42:8 (ESV)

[8] I am the LORD; that is my name; my glory I give to no other, nor my praise to carved idols.

God said He would not share with or give any of His glory or praise to anyone or anything. God will not share His glory or praise with a graven image or an idol. God said He will not tolerate your affection for any other gods (graven images or idols). This means and includes all statues or pictures of any likeness of any sort that we might or would bow down to. Likeness means anything that would resemble or depict God or Jesus or a man or a woman or represent any type of animal. God said lest (lest: for fear of not preventing oneself from being corrupted, or for fear of doing something undesirable) for fear that we might become corrupt by making a graven image or idol, that we might love and worship, thinking of it as God.

The Bible does not tell us what Jesus Christ looks like. So! Who is that guy in the picture that people claim to be Jesus? Do you have any affection for him? Any graven image of God or Jesus Christ or likeness of them is not approved by God. Religions break the first three commandments when they have statues or pictures that they bow down to before they start to pray to God. Think about it the next time you go to church and you bow down to pray and there is a statue or picture in front of you. Are you bowing down before a graven image? Do you start to talk to it as if you are talking to God or as if it would help you to get to God? Is its likeness as if you were talking to God or someone else? Do you feel that because you are looking up to it as you pray, God is hearing your prayers better? Do you feel that the statue is in the likeness of who you think it is while you are praying? If your answer is yes to any of these questions, then you are sharing God's glory with that statue or picture and breaking the first three commandments.

Think about it—are you obeying a religion, or are you obeying God's Word? Read the first three commandments again and think about it. God does not want us to make any graven image or idol of any likeness of man, woman, or animal of any sort. God does not and will not share His glory and praise with anyone else or with any graven image or idol. God does not approve of anyone worshipping Him by bowing down before any graven image or idol of any likeness of any sort. God said He would not tolerate our affection for them. If you think that I am not in agreement with God's Word on graven images and idols, then read Exodus 20:3-5; Deuteronomy 5:7-9; Deuteronomy 4:16-17; and Isaiah 42:8 again. I believe I have it right on what God said in the Bible.

Side note: There are two major religions that do not view or believe Exodus 20:4 and Deuteronomy 5:8 is the second commandment of the ten commandments. They also believe Exodus 20:17 and Deuteronomy 5:21 is the ninth and tenth commandment when, actually, the whole verse of Exodus 20:17

and Deuteronomy 5:21 is the tenth commandment. If you will open your Bible and carefully read Deuteronomy chapter 4:11 through 25. These verses confirm and expound on the second commandment that it is about graven images; Exodus 20:4 and Deuteronomy 5:8 is the second commandment. Now, let's move on. According to the scholars, Isaiah chapter 53 talks about Christ. If you look in your Bible, verse 5 verifies that this chapter is talking about Jesus Christ. Verse 2 is the only biblical account of Christ Jesus' appearance of what He may have looked like before/or after His death and resurrection.

Isaiah 53:2 (NLT)

² My servant grew up in the LORD'S presence like a tender green shoot, like a root in dry ground. There was nothing beautiful or majestic about his appearance, nothing to attract us to him.

There was nothing beautiful or majestic about His appearance, nothing to attract us to Him. This description does not fit, or even come close to, the picture of the man that people think is Jesus. That picture is not Jesus. It is merely an artist's rendering. If you have any affection for the man in that picture because you believe or think He is Jesus, then you need to read Exodus 20:5 and Deuteronomy 5:9, 4:16–17 again.

Deuteronomy 4:16–17 (NIV)

¹⁶ So that you do not become corrupt and make for yourselves an idol, an image of any shape, whether formed like a man or a woman,

> [17] or like any animal on earth or any bird that flies in the air.

God will not share His glory with an image of any shape, whether formed like a man, a woman, an animal, or a bird. God does not want us to bow down and worship or pray to these images. God will not tolerate our affection for them. When we bow down to worship God, and there is a graven image in front of us, we are giving glory to that graven image. When we have any love or affection for that graven image, we are giving glory to it. Again, God said He would *not* share or give His glory or praise to any graven image. He will not tolerate our affection for them.

"Is it wrong to have pictures and statues?" No, just as long as you do not praise, worship, or pray to them. And you do not use them for making a connection with God or thinking of them as gods or as God Himself. There is a difference between regular pictures and statues and what God calls graven images. God considers a picture and a statue to be a graven image or idol when people bow down before them to praise and worship God or to praise and worship them; when people bow down before them to pray to them or to pray to God; when people show or have love and affection for the image with the thought of this is what or whom they are praising and worshipping or praying to; when people are relating to them as their being connected to God as they worship Him; when people look at the image or hold the image as if it will help them to get their prayers answered.

Pictures and statues are graven images and idols only when they are being worshipped or being used for any type or form of worship. If people have a graven image or idol that is used for any type of worship, even if the people are not using them for worship they are still a graven image or idol. Why? Because the graven images and idols were originally made for worship. There are those who will say, "We do not worship them." But they still bow down before them to worship God, thinking they will not be corrupted by them. God does not want us to have graven images or idols, whether we worship them or not.

God tells us if we have or make for ourselves an idol, an image of any shape, whether formed like a man or a woman, or like any animal on earth or any bird that flies in the air, that this may corrupt us. We should *not* have these things before us or in front of us when we praise, worship, or pray to God. He will not share His glory with them and will not tolerate our love and affection for them.

"Mike, what about the fish symbol, the cross, or the crucifix?" The crucifix has too much of a tenancy to corrupt us to worship it because it is a graven image of a man who is supposed to be Jesus. That is a graven image of God. Plus, Jesus should not be looked upon as being on the cross because He is alive and dwells in us. In the Old Testament, the Jews had symbols of their tribes and symbols that stated their beliefs in God, which God never spoke against. The fish symbol and the cross without the crucifix are symbols that state we believe in God and follow Jesus Christ. We never did and do not use them as objects of or for worship.

"Mike, are the statues of a nativity scene graven images or idols?" This is a fine line. I would have to say yes and no. I cannot speak for others, but I do not worship those statues, nor do I bow down before a nativity scene for worship. They are an object of celebration showing and reminding us of how humble Jesus Christ the King has entered into the world. It is saying we believe in what is being said about the birth of Jesus Christ. The statues are nothing more than a representation of Mary, Joseph, and Jesus as a baby. I personally have no love or affection for the statues of the nativity scene because they are just statues.

When it comes to the nativity scene, there is a fine line on whether the statues are graven images and idols or not. This is a touchy subject. Here, I will only give an answer of opinion according to the understanding of the commandment. If people believe the statues of the nativity scene really are Mary, Joseph, and Jesus or have any affection for the statues as Mary, Joseph, and Jesus, then they are graven images or idols. If people believe the statues are not really Mary, Joseph, and Jesus but just a representation of them and have no love or affection for them, then they are not considered graven images or idols. What do the Scriptures say? This is one where you have to decide for yourself where you stand on your personal belief of these statues.

If people use pictures and statues to worship, believing they are helping them to connect with God, then the pictures and statues do become graven images or idols. Graven images and idols do not and cannot connect people to God. Nor can they or do they draw people nearer to God. If people say a picture or statue is God or Jesus and have any love or affection for them, then they are graven images and idols. Why? Because people are making them a god or making them to be God by what they are doing and by what they believe about them.

I may be repeating myself, but I want to be clearly understood on what makes a picture, statue, or object become a graven image or idol. Pictures, statues, and objects also become graven images and idols when people think or believe these things have the power to answer prayer or the power to ward off evil. Believing in any way that these things can keep them safe makes them graven images and idols. In conclusion, graven images and idols are pictures and statues that people believe are to be God and Jesus or believe that they are a god and bow down before them to worship them, or for worshipping God, believing they can make or have a stronger connection with God through them.

God does not want us to bow down before graven images or idols to worship Him, and He will not tolerate our love and affection for them.

CHAPTER 18:

THE IMPORTANCE OF WORSHIPPING GOD AND BEING ON TIME

Before I start on praise and worship, I want to make a statement. Just because a church does not worship exactly the way the Bible teaches, it does not mean that those worshipping are not born again. If a church does worship exactly the way the Bible teaches, but it is not from the heart, that church may be saved, but God still will not be pleased because they do not worship with all their heart. No church is perfect.

Unfortunately, not all Christian churches worship or can worship exactly the way the Bible teaches (some churches just don't have the instrumentalists), and you are not going to find the perfect church because we are not perfect. No matter who you are, if you find a perfect church, the moment you start attending it, that church will no longer be perfect.

This chapter is not to judge churches or others as to how they worship God, but rather to judge ourselves as to whether or not we are worshipping God in the way God says we should worship Him. Please keep this in mind as you read this chapter. How will everyone know what God expects when there is not enough teaching on how to worship God? Here are a few ways to look at what is being taught here. "Well, I know that," or "Oh good, I am doing the right things in worshipping God." Or "Ouch and oops, I did not know that, and I need to change some of the ways I worship God." Remember, this is not for anyone to judge anyone's church; we all have our faults. This chapter is to judge our own praise and worship. Now, let's see what the Bible says.

Worship God because God loves to be worshipped. God deserves our worship, and God is worthy of our worship. Praise is an act of worship. Remember I said God tells us what He wants us to do and what He does not want us to do; it is all in the Bible. It is the same with worship.

"Mike, how does God want us to worship Him?" We will look at some of the many verses that will answer your question.

Psalm 47:1, 6–7 (KJV)

¹ O clap your hands, all ye people; shout unto God with the voice of triumph.

⁶ ...Sing praises to God, sing praises: sing praises unto our King, sing praises.

⁷ For God is the King of all the earth: sing ye praises with understanding.

Ephesians 5:18–20 (NIV)

¹⁸ Do not get drunk on wine, which leads to debauchery. Instead, be filled with the Spirit,

¹⁹ speaking to one another with psalms, hymns, and songs from the Spirit. Sing and make music from your heart to the Lord,

²⁰ always giving thanks to God the Father for everything, in the name of our Lord Jesus Christ.

Psalm 112:1 (NIV)

¹ Praise the LORD. Blessed are those who fear the LORD, who find great delight in his commands.

God's Word says clap your hands, all you nations; shout to God with cries of joy, shout with the voice of triumph. God wants us to clap our hands and shout with a voice of triumph when we worship Him. Sing praises, psalms, hymns, and spiritual songs. Speak out to one another in psalms and hymns, which means we can hear each other as we sing. We are to praise Him with thanksgiving in our hearts. When we delight ourselves in the Lord and His commandments, we are greatly blessed, worshipping Him with all our heart. As we worship, we are to revere God. Revere means to show honor and devotion to God. We are to sing and make music in our heart to the Lord. God wants to hear us (yes!). God wants to hear us sing to Him.

You could say the next few paragraphs are my pet peeve because of what I am stating in them. Because of the things I'm about to tell you, I found it hard to focus on my own praise and worship and, therefore, difficult to enjoy worship. As head usher in a church that I was in, I had other people complain to me about the same things. I'm sure this does not happen all the time or in every church.

In reading the Bible, one comes to realize that God wants things done in order.

There is a time for everything. A time to sing, a time to shout, and a time to clap your hands. There is nothing more disturbing to those who are singing when one or more people start to shout out loud the words that they think God or other people should hear while they should be singing with the others. God wants us to worship Him in harmony. Worship leaders are to lead us in what we are supposed to be doing during praise and worship. Why have someone leading us in singing praises if we are going to do our own thing and not follow the leader's lead? It is not okay when someone shouts and interrupts others with their preaching or shouting while the others are trying to enjoy the singing of songs to the Lord. That is not how it works; we all are supposed to sing along with the worship leader or leaders.

I am not saying be quiet, don't shout. I am saying there is a time when, and I mean when, to shout and yell out loud praises (not preach; the pastor will preach later to the people) to the Lord. I did not say be quiet in your praise and worship, I said do it in an orderly fashion.

For those who feel their voices are too quiet when they are singing, their voice will be heard by God even if it is not louder than the others. If you clap your hands, do not clap them so loud as to stand out from the others during the song. At the end of a song or songs, you can clap and shout as loud as you want to clap and shout, to praise and glorify the Lord. If you want to clap your hands during the song, then clap to the beat of the music. But of course, if your church does not do all or any of that, do not push it. Follow the way your church worship leader or leaders lead you. Change should never come from a pew in the church but from the pulpit and the church should be in agreement with the change.

Yes, we should sing and shout with a voice of triumph in the sanctuary, but we should do it in harmony, following the lead of the worship leader or leaders.

> Deuteronomy 10:12 (NIV)
>
> ¹² And now, Israel, what does the LORD your God ask of you but to fear the LORD your God, to walk in obedience to him, to love him, to serve the LORD your God with all your heart and with all your soul.

Deuteronomy 10:12 is to help us understand the reverence and godly fear that is mentioned in the following verses.

> Hebrews 12:28 (AMP)
>
> ²⁸ Let us therefore, receiving a kingdom that is firm and stable and cannot be shaken, offer to God pleasing service and acceptable worship, with modesty and pious care and godly fear and awe.

> Revelation 14:7 (NIV)
>
> ⁷ He said in a loud voice, "Fear God and give him glory, because the hour of his judgment has come. Worship him who made the heavens, the earth, the sea and the springs of water."

As we read in Psalm 112:1, "Blessed is the man that fears the Lord, he that delights greatly in His commandments." God is saying we are blessed if (there is that big "if" again) we godly fear Him and greatly delight in His commandments. We are not to fear God as to be afraid of Him (not like, oh no, it's God!), but to have a godly fear of reverence towards Him. It is not to be a fear of terror. There is a difference. As we read in Deuteronomy 10:12, God requires us to fear Him by walking in all His ways, to love Him, and to serve Him with all our heart and with all our soul.

We are to serve Him with all our heart and with all our soul. This does not mean that we have to start serving God in a church. We can serve God in many ways, but if we just got saved, God wants us to learn first. If we have been saved for a while, it won't hurt to volunteer once in a while if your church needs help. Especially if your church is asking for volunteers. Having said what I just said, a church does need people serving in it. To serve in a church is a good thing to do.

In Hebrews 12:28 and Revelation 14:7, fear God by obeying His commandments and give Him glory and reverence by praising and worshipping Him. These verses talk about fearing God and worshipping God as one subject. Fear God by giving Him glory because His judgment is here. We are to fear God's judgment and His wrath. We are to have a fear of being disobedient to God because of His wrath because being disobedient is sin, and sin separates us from God.

God requires us to worship Him. Worshipping God is not an option. God wants us to give Him glory and praise, to worship Him with reverence and awe. God is worthy of everything that He wants from us and of us because He saved us from hell and gave us eternal life.

Psalm 150:1–6 (NIV)

[1] Praise the LORD. Praise God in his sanctuary; praise him in his mighty heavens.

[2] Praise him for his acts of power; praise him for his surpassing greatness.

³ Praise him with the sounding of the trumpet, praise him with the harp and lyre,

⁴ praise him with timbrel and dancing, praise him with strings and pipe,

⁵ praise him with the clash of cymbals, praise him with resounding cymbals.

⁶ Let everything that has breath praise the LORD. Praise the LORD.

Hebrews 10:25 (KJV)

²⁵ Not forsaking the assembling of ourselves together, as the manner of some is; but exhorting one another: and so much the more, as ye see the day approaching.

We are not to forsake the assembling of ourselves together. Because we need the fellowship and support of our brothers and sisters in the Lord.

Before I start talking about worshipping in the sanctuary, I want to say that I am not saying you cannot worship God in your home or somewhere else. People say, "Well, I can worship Him at home or anywhere I am," but how often will the average person worship God at home or somewhere else? Not very, and worshipping God at home or somewhere else is not the same as when we assemble together. Taking Psalm 150 as a whole, it is talking about worshipping in a sanctuary. Keep this in mind as I talk about worshipping God in His sanctuary and not at home or somewhere else.

I was told by a believer that he/she believes their body is the sanctuary. I do not believe that is the sanctuary that is being talked about in Psalm 150 unless everyone knows how to play all of these instruments, or they can have all those instruments in their body. Like Psalm 150, I am talking about the sanctuary that people assemble in. Hebrews 10:25 (KJV), "25 Not forsaking the assembling of ourselves together."

Whenever we think of a sanctuary, we think of a room that has pews and an altar; we think of a place of worship. We are to praise God in His sanctuary, in church. God wants us to worship Him in His sanctuary. To worship God in His sanctuary means that we should go to church. God wants us to worship Him with a lot of different types of instruments and to dance to Him in worship. So! When we see a church that worships God with music and dancing, this does not mean that they are worshipping Him wrongly. As we read in Psalm 150, that is what God wants. God does not want us to just think joy, but to be joyful and to show our joy to Him when we worship Him.

I want to make some suggestions. Do not leave your church just because they are not worshipping the way it is written in Psalm 150. If no one dances in your church, that does not mean they are not worshipping right. If you want to dance, I feel that maybe you should find a church that does not object to dancing in church. If your church allows dancing, do dance appropriately. Does God want you to show Him your joy when you are worshipping Him? Yes! God does not want you to just stand and sing with a straight face, looking dead to Him. He not only wants to hear your joy, but He wants to see your joy. "Mike, do people dance in your church?" No, but some do move a little bit, and so do I. Not all of us stand still. Some may feel uncomfortable dancing to God because they have never done it, and we must take that into consideration. Do not judge anyone's praise and worship; God does that. Judge your own praise and worship according to the Bible.

I do want to say that do not think wrongly of a person's worship if they do not dance. The same goes for one that does dance. If God did not want us to dance to Him in church, it would not be in the Bible. It is not for us to decide if a person is worshipping God wrongly or not, that is up to God. But God does want it to be taught and wants us to worship Him correctly.

Philippians 4:4 (NIV)

⁴ Rejoice in the Lord always. I will say it again: Rejoice!

Again, Psalm 150:2, "Praise God for His excellent greatness, according to the abundance of His greatness, for His surpassing greatness."

Praise and worship God with enthusiasm. Praise God for creating you and saving you from hell and for the things that He does for you in your life.

Now, when you go to a game of any sport or watch any sport on TV, you do not worship them, but you do praise your team when they score and when they win. When you go to a concert or a performance of any sort, and you enjoy it, you do not worship them, but you praise them for how well they performed, you clap your hands, and you are full of joy. Your face has a very big smile. If you are at a concert or a performance, you will stand and clap your hands and shout for them. If it is a game or a concert, you will jump up and down for them and cheer them on. Rejoicing in what they have done for you. Do you behave this way towards God when you are praising Him, or do you stand there in church with a straight face, outwardly showing no signs of joy? Oops, or should I say ouch? Do you do the same for God or not? Only God and you know the answers to these questions.

I was once told by a believer that if you show your emotions while you are worshipping and praising God, that means you are basing your salvation on your emotions. That you are getting into emotionalism. I have never, and will never, base my salvation on my emotions when I dance and have a smile from ear to ear while worshipping the Lord our God. Get real! If God wanted us to have somber, sour-puss-looking faces, God would not have said to worship Him with a lot of instruments in song and dance. This is not emotionalism. Psalm 150 sounds like a joyful and exciting time to me. Not a time to have a sour puss look on your face—where it looks like your face has been dipped in pickle juice. Nowhere in the Bible does it say to not show your emotions to God. Nor does it say to have a straight face while worshipping Him so that you do not base your salvation on your emotions.

If God thought we would base our salvation on our emotions as we showed them while worshipping Him, He would not have given us certain songs. One of them is, "Get all excited, go tell everybody! That Jesus Christ is King!" This song is to be sung with enthusiasm. "Get all excited," that does not sound like "don't show your emotions." I also don't think Psalm 150 would be in the Bible either if we were not to show our emotions. How can you not show any emotions if you worship God the way it is written in Psalm 150? There are hundreds of verses that tell us to sing and be joyful to the Lord in worshipping Him. Showing your emotions to God when you're worshipping Him is not getting into emotionalism. It is showing God that you love Him and that you are excited about Him.

During the praise and worship at church we are to sing to God. God wants to hear us singing to Him. "Mike, I do not sound good, and I cannot sing." That does not matter; God still wants to hear your voice. What matters to God is that He hears you worshipping Him. Worship God with all of your heart. Give God all the glory and all the praise. God knows that not everyone can sing, but He still wants to hear everyone. Now, if you have a physical health problem, then that is a different story. God understands if you have a physical health problem that makes it difficult for you to sing or dance. I am not saying you better sing and dance or else, but at least outwardly show God your joy. It is good to enjoy the praise and worship, but that is not what you are in church for. You are in church for God to enjoy your praise and worship to Him.

God is looking for true worshippers. Jesus is the one speaking in the following two verses.

John 4:23-24 (NIV)

[23] Yet a time is coming and has now come when the true worshipers will worship the Father in the Spirit and in truth, for they are the kind of worshipers the Father seeks [the Father is looking for].

[24] God is spirit, and his worshipers must worship in the Spirit and in truth.

You must worship God in spirit and in truth. The truth is God's Word. God wants us to worship Him in His truth, the way the Bible says to worship Him.

> Deuteronomy 6:4–6 (NLT)
>
> ⁴ Listen, O Israel! The LORD is our God, the LORD alone.
>
> ⁵ And you must love the Lord your God with all your heart, all your soul, and all your strength.
>
> ⁶ And you must commit yourselves wholeheartedly to these commands that I am giving you today.

God wants you to commit yourselves wholeheartedly to Him with all that you are. This is a command from God to all of us. Remember, God created you. He gave you life here on Earth. God gave you Jesus Christ, His only Son, so you could have eternal life in heaven. God the Father loves you. God the Son loves you. God the Holy Spirit loves you. Therefore, when you worship God, commit all of your love to Him. Worship God with all your heart in spirit and in truth. Show God that you love Him when you worship Him.

The other point that I want to bring out in John 4:23-24 is that God is looking for or seeking true worshippers. I feel God wants me to point out the qualities or things that He is looking for in a true worshipper. Mainly because *God is looking* for true worshippers.

> Romans 12:1–2 (KJV)
>
> ¹ I beseech you therefore, brethren, by the mercies of God, that ye present your bodies a living sacrifice, holy, acceptable unto God, which is your reasonable service.

² And be not conformed to this world: but be ye transformed by the renewing of your mind, that ye may prove what is that good, and acceptable, and perfect, will of God.

These two verses give just some of the characteristics of a true worshiper. It is one who presents their body as a living sacrifice, holy and acceptable to God. One who is not conformed to this world but is transformed by the renewing of their mind. The renewing of the mind helps one to be able to discern or prove what is the good, acceptable, and perfect will of God.

Here are some desires that a true worshiper may have. When a true worshiper goes on vacation away from home, they look for a church that is like their church and go to it. A true worshiper desires to go to church and worship God. A true worshiper will do what it takes to be at church on time. A true worshiper will not leave the sanctuary until the service is over unless it is really necessary.

God loves you! And wants you to be a true worshiper. He wants to hear all of us singing to Him in His sanctuary. But how can God hear you sing to Him in His sanctuary if you are not in the sanctuary during the praise and song part of the service? If your singing to God in the sanctuary was not important to God, He would not have it in the Bible. God looks at our heart, are we focused on Him?

Before I continue, I have to say a few things. I am not trying to be judgmental or trying to judge. Some will say I am, but I am pointing out all the nitpicking facts on the following subject in order to establish and cover all the points. This is a touchy subject, and for some, this will be an "ouch." If you are being addressed on this subject, only you and God will know. This subject is too touchy to address someone on a one-to-one basis. If this offends you, I am sorry. But because of how often this is happening in the churches today, it needs to be addressed. God did not tell me to go easy on this. In order to love someone, you must have feelings. "God is love," God has feelings (1 John 4:8). As you read the following, think of God's commands, love, and feelings, which need to be taken into consideration to help you understand why I am addressing the following subject in this chapter. We really need to try to look at this from the point of view that God might have on this, with the aspect of us being obedient to God.

Singing in the sanctuary is not for our entertainment. It is for the sole purpose of praising, worshipping, magnifying, and glorifying God.

Using John 4:23–24, along with what I wrote earlier about worship, God and I want to address those who come late to church all the time. From some, I have heard, "Well, God understands." Yes, you are right; God does understand. What God understands is that when you come late, you interrupt the praise and worship of those who came on time. God understands you interrupt the usher's praise and worship. One of the usher's duties is to seat people when they come into the sanctuary. When a person (or persons) comes in late after the usher has found seating (nine times out of ten), the usher most likely has to interrupt someone else's praise and worship to get the latecomers seated. God understands when you come late all the time that singing praises to Him is not that important to you.

When you go to a game of any sport or watch any sport on TV, or when you go to a live concert or a live performance of any sort, you usually get there on time. In fact, you get there early to be seated before it starts so you don't miss anything. You also do the same thing when you go to a movie. God understands that being on time or early for these things and not for Him makes these things more important to you than He is. "Ouch!" God understands that He is a lower priority on your list than all the other things when you come in late all the time to worship Him.

Let us not forget about work; we have to be on time for work. No matter how many millions of things (of excuses) we have to do to get ready before going to work, we get there on time most or all of the time. Coming to church, these same excuses make us late all the time. There are no good excuses for being late for church all the time; the answer is: get up earlier. How can we expect God to do something for us if we cannot give God one complete hour of our time each week to worship Him and to hear the message that God has for us that week? Being on time for church means being in the sanctuary before the service starts and being ready to worship God. Singing songs of praise and worship to God in the sanctuary is important to God. It is also an important part of being born again.

"Mike, you do not understand I have kids/I have problems." My wife and I had three excuses of our own. I love my boys. Two were in diapers at the same time. As they got older, we made sure they were ready the night before. My boys were not the only excuses. Over the years, countless excuses have come up. We fought the excuses, won the battles, and made it to church on time. One of the things we did was get up earlier until it was early enough. Satan has millions of excuses for us to be late for church.

What examples are we setting for new believers? What do they think when we come late all the time? God wants us to be good examples for others. Getting to church on time is one of these good examples.

What I also want to talk about in John 4:23-24 is that God was and still is seeking and looking for true worshipers. Do you consider yourself a true worshiper? Think about your worship to God, ask yourself, am I a true worshiper? Worship means to pray and to sing; yes, sing to God. God wants all of us to sing together in His sanctuary to Him. It is very important to God that we all sing to Him. If it were not important to God, the book of Psalms would not be in the Bible.

If you are committed to God, I think that maybe God does understand your coming late, if you have a job that will not let you go until the last minute. Or if you have to leave before the service is over because of a job (a place of work) or a job that you have to take care of immediately once the service ends. God does understand.

People will go to a concert for two or three hours and not leave until the last song is done. They also go to a sporting event that will last three hours or more and stay until it is done, yet they have to leave before the one-hour service is over.

God wants us to sing psalms and hymns making music in our hearts to Him. To fully do that in church, we have to get into the music and sing with all our hearts while we focus on God. To do that, we have to be in the sanctuary on time. When a person comes in late all the time, it interrupts someone else's praise and worship. I believe God wants us to be in church on time. Having said all that, if you cannot help being late, still come to church anyway. The Bible teaches that God knows all and sees all. God knows our priorities on praise and worship in church. Does God think of a person as a true worshipper when he or she comes to church late all the time? I don't know, but if He does not, ouch! God understands when a person comes late *all* the time that they do not make an effort to overcome all the different excuses. God understands that no matter what the excuse is, worshipping Him is just not that important to them. Get up earlier. It is better to be early or really early than to be late all the time. Things do not always go right, but I still make it to church on time. Ask God to help you to overcome the problems. God wants to see you and hear your singing, your praises, and your worship to Him. When church is over, the question is, was God pleased with your worship? I know we all want the answer to be yes.

When you go to church, God is watching. He searches your heart looking for your praises to Him. He wants to hear your voice singing praises to Him. "Who, little old nothing me? I am just another nobody, why would He want to hear my voice?" Because to God, you are somebody, God loves you, and you mean a lot to Him. If God did not care about you, then Jesus Christ would not have died for you. Your praise and worship are important to God. "Who me?" Yes, you, your praise and worship are important to God.

Note: This paragraph is for those who cannot sing. I cannot sing, nor do I sound good when I sing, but I sing to God anyway because God tells us to sing praises to Him. If you do not sound good, don't worry about it; sing anyway. God will still enjoy it because you are singing praises to Him. He wants to hear you sing praises to Him no matter how bad of a singer you are; God will enjoy your singing to Him. Like I said earlier, if you have a physical health problem that keeps you from singing, then that is a different story. God understands.

I have been asked, "What did you do with all the money?"

I said, "What money?"

The reply was, "The money that your mom gave you for singing lessons?"

I said, "I spent it on candy."

God is still looking for true worshippers, and if you are not one already, He is looking for you to become one. "You mean me?" Yes, you! God wants you to be a true worshipper. He is looking for you because He loves you.

What the bottom line of worship is, as my pastor put it, it is not all about you. Worship is not about you being entertained or how much you enjoyed it. Whether you sang, danced, or clapped your hands or not. If your worship did not come from your heart to God, then it was not worship. Worship is magnifying and glorifying God. When the service is over, it is not whether or not you had a good time. Yes, you can have and should have a good time in worship. The real question is, did you please God during the whole service or not? Was God pleased with your worship and your attitude towards Him or not? At the end of the service, can God say, "I was truly worshipped"? That is what worshipping God is all about.

You can only get out of a worship service of what you put in it. If you put little or nothing into it, you will get little or nothing out of it. If you put a lot into it, you will get a lot out of it. It depends on you if God will fill you with His joy or not while you are worshipping Him. It depends on you if you get something out of the message that can help you in life. If every message that a pastor preaches tickles your ears, then the pastor is not doing his job. A good pastor will step on your toes from time to time in a message. But it will not be the pastor who is stepping on your toes; it will be the Holy Spirit stepping on your toes through the message that the pastor is preaching. Getting your toes stepped on occasionally in a message is a good thing. Yes, we do need to have our ears tickled in a message from time to time, too.

Singing to God is just one of the ways of praising and worshipping Him. No matter what the reason is or how one feels, God wants us there for the song part of the service and not just for the message.

Be a true worshipper, come to church and be in the sanctuary on time. Be a doer of the Word. God wants to hear you sing to Him in the sanctuary. God wants to see your love and joy for Him when you worship Him. Worship God with all your heart. God loves you and wants you to be a true worshipper. A reminder: You are very important to God. For God so loved the world. For God so loved you that He gave you His only Son.

CHAPTER 19:

What Does God Say about Judging Others?

Jesus is the one speaking in the following verses.

Matthew 7:1–5 (NIV)

¹ Do not judge, or you too will be judged.

² For in the same way you judge others, you will be judged, and with the measure you use, it will be measured to you.

³ Why do you look at the speck of sawdust in your brother's eye and pay no attention to the plank in your own eye?

⁴ How can you say to your brother, 'Let me take the speck out of your eye,' when all the time there is a plank in your own eye?

⁵ You hypocrite, first take the plank out of your own eye, and then you will see clearly to remove the speck from your brother's eye.

If you do not want to be judged by others, then do not judge others. When you judge others, whatever way you judge them, you will be judged in that same way. These verses are clear: do not judge other people; God will do that when the time comes.

Never think you are better because you are smarter or have much more than someone else. Never think that you are much better because you are born again or because you go to church and you are reading the Bible and doing the will of God. Never think that you are much better than someone else for whatever reason, period!

If you do think that you are better than someone else and look down at others, then you need to get the beam of timber or the plank out of your own eye first before you attempt to get the speck out of your brother's eye. This also includes what we think of unbelievers as well. We need to help the unbelievers to understand what it means to be born again in a loving way. God does not want us to force the unbeliever to believe. Never try to do that.

"Mike, what does judging others have to do with understanding what it means to be born again?" All of God's commands are a part of understanding what it means to be born again. As you read earlier, as born-again believers, we are to go out into the world and preach the gospel. I have seen too many believers judge one another, and this hurts helping an unbeliever to become born again (saved). We forget that we are not to judge but rather to help each believer get back on their feet again when they fall. Some believers judge too much and do not see the planks in their own eyes. When we see a believer fall to sin, we should lovingly help them get right with God again.

I have also seen the believer judge the unbeliever. I, too, was guilty of that. We forget we were once there ourselves and that sin has control over the unbeliever. It is easy for Satan to get the unbeliever to do bad things.

We forget that we are not to judge the unbeliever but to be a witness for God and help the unbeliever to come to God. Do not judge a sinner, but instead, show them the way to God, for we have all sinned and fallen short of the glory of God. We have to remember that we are human and, as humans, we do make mistakes.

I have seen ministers of God be judged by others and never forgiven because they made a mistake. We have to remember that they, too, are human and not perfect. Just as God forgives, we are required to forgive. It is a bad witness for God when anyone who says they are born again continues to live a life of sin, especially if they are a spiritual leader in church. If they repent, God will forgive them.

If a minister or a church leader of any kind constantly sins or continues to live a lifestyle of sin, they should not stay in a position of authority in the church. They should repent, turn away from their sin, and step down from their position of authority. God will not honor nor anoint a church leader of any kind who constantly sins or continues to live a lifestyle of sin. "Mike, if a minister repents, turns away from their sin, and steps down for retribution, would God restore that minister to their ministry?" Yes, I have seen it happen. After a period of time, God restored the minister to his ministry. Never expect a spiritual leader to be perfect because none of us are perfect.

When a person of high standing in the church falls to sin, do not be quick to judge. Too often, we do just that and forget that the person is human and can make mistakes. Are any of us so perfect as to not fall into the same temptation? No! Instead of saying with an attitude, "Well, I never," we should try to see what we can do to help that person to restore themselves back to God. If a person needs to be judged by the law, then let the law judge that person.

When a person of high stature falls to sin, we treat them like a scumbag. When a person of very low stature does the same thing, we don't think much of it and try to help them become a better person. No matter what the person's status is, they should all be treated the same. They should be held accountable for what they did wrong. If they repent and strive not to do it again, we should be like God and forgive them. If the law requires a punishment, the person should still take their punishment. Just as God forgave and forgives us, we should forgive others.

When pointing out what is sin according to the Bible, people will say you are judging. How will anyone know if their lifestyle is sinful or not if it is not pointed out according to biblical teaching? Two simple examples: Someone says to a thief, "The Bible says you should not steal," and to a killer, "The Bible says you should not kill." Their response is, "Oh, you're judging." No, you are not judging; you are just pointing out what sin is according to the Bible. It is never easy to show a correction or what is sin without offending someone or coming across as if you are judging them. In many cases, correction does convict and condemn us, for our hearts are convicting us because we are being shown what we are doing wrong. When we sin against God, corrections are to help us see what we are doing wrong so we can be led into repentance and to help us do what is right.

Like it or not, everyone has judged someone at one time or another and more than once, but remember, none of us is without sin. God hates sin, but He *loves* the sinner. John 3:16–17 (paraphrased by the author), "For God so loved the sinner that

He gave His Son's life to the sinner so whoever believes might be saved. God did not send His Son to condemn the sinner, but to save the sinner." "Might be saved" because each of us has to receive Jesus individually.

When you judge, you never know when you will be judged. Remember—do not judge others, for you will be judged in that same way. None of us is perfect, and we all have feelings. Do not expect to be treated right by others if you cannot treat others right.

There is a lot more to learn about judging but I only talked about the aspect of judging on what God wanted me to talk about.

CHAPTER 20:

THE THREE BEING ONE GOD (THE TRINITY)

The word trinity is not in the Bible. We use the word trinity to describe the three-in-one God. A belief that is sort of understood when you are reading the Bible. "Mike, why do you say sort of understood?" Because even after you see that they are three in one, or the one is three, it is still mind-boggling trying to figure out how the three are one or the one can be three. There are verses in the Bible that show us that God is Jesus and that Jesus Christ is God. There are verses that give us a very good indication that the Holy Spirit is God and is Jesus, that the three are one, which is why we call them the Trinity. I, for one, believe in the Trinity. As you read and study the Bible, you will see that God, Jesus, and the Holy Spirit have, if you will, different roles or positions in our lives, but They are still one. Even though they are three individuals, they still are one God.

I fully believe that God is Jesus Christ and the Holy Spirit. That Jesus Christ is God and the Holy Spirit. That the Holy Spirit is God and Jesus Christ. I will be showing only a small portion of verses that show and prove that the three are one God.

In different parts of the Bible Jesus claims the same attributes that God has, making Himself to be equal to God and/or claiming to be God. The Jewish leaders and elders understood this, and that is why they tried to stone Jesus and wanted Him dead because they did not believe Him.

Exodus 3:14 (NIV)

[14] God said to Moses, "I AM WHO I AM. This is what you are to say to the Israelites: 'I AM has sent me to you!'"

John 8:53-59 (NIV)

[53] "Are you greater than our father Abraham? He died, and so did the prophets. Who do you think you are?"

[54] Jesus replied, "If I glorify myself, my glory means nothing. My Father, whom you claim as your God, is the one who glorifies me.

[55] Though you do not know him, I know him. If I said I did not, I would be a liar like you, but I do know him and obey his word.

[56] Your father Abraham rejoiced at the thought of seeing my day; he saw it and was glad."

[57] "You are not yet fifty years old," they said to him, "and you have seen Abraham!"

[58] "Very truly I tell you," Jesus answered, "before Abraham was born, I am!"

[59] At this, they picked up stones to stone him, but Jesus hid himself, slipping away from the temple grounds.

In John chapter 8, starting with verse 19, Jesus was telling the Jews that they did not know God, His Father, because of their unbelief in Him. The Jewish leaders then asked Jesus, "Are You greater than our father Abraham and the prophets of those who are all dead? Who do You think You are?" In answering the Jews, Jesus called the Jews liars because, according to Jesus, the Jews did not know God like they claimed they did. In verse 56, Jesus talks about Abraham as though He had talked to Abraham when Abraham was alive. The Jews were totally shocked in disbelief and said, "You are not even fifty years old; how could You have seen or talked to Abraham?" Jesus answered them by identifying Himself, referring to Exodus 3:14 by saying, "Before Abraham was born, I am!"

When Moses asked God, "Who should I say sent me?" God identified Himself as I AM. "Say, I AM has sent me to you." The Jews knew and understood that when Jesus said, "I AM," He was claiming that He is God, the I AM. The Jews knew and understood that Jesus was referring to Exodus 3:14 when He said, "I AM." That is why they picked up stones to stone Him. They thought, *How dare He make such a claim! Who does He think He is?* They were sure that Jesus was not God.

In Isaiah 9:6 (NIV) (emphasis added by the author), we are told the names of Jesus, identifying who He is,

> ⁶ For to us a child is born, to us a son is given, and the government will be on his shoulders. And he will be called Wonderful Counselor, *Mighty God, Everlasting Father,* Prince of Peace.

Chapter 20: The Three Being One God (the Trinity)

I put in italics *Mighty God* and *Everlasting Father* because God the Father is called the Mighty God and the Everlasting Father, and Jesus here is not being called the Son, but He is being called the Mighty God and the Everlasting Father. This is showing that not only is Jesus God the Son, but that He is God the Father.

Let's read what Jesus said in John 17:5 (NIV)

⁵ And now, Father, glorify me in your presence with the glory I had with you before the world began.

Looking at Isaiah 9:6 (KJV), "6 For unto us a child is born, unto us a son is given." This is definitely talking about Jesus. Two of the names that Jesus will be and is called definitely identify Him as God, "Mighty God, Everlasting Father." In John 17:5, Jesus asked God the Father to glorify Him with the glory He had with God before the world began. As we read earlier, God will not share His glory with anyone, but God does share His glory with Jesus. God shares His glory with (God) Jesus Himself because Jesus is God (mind-boggling, but true).

In Revelation 1:8; 22:13, Jesus is the one who is doing the talking.

Revelation 1:8 (NIV)

⁸ "I am the Alpha and the Omega," says the Lord God, "who is, and who was, and who is to come, the Almighty."

> Revelation 22:13 (NIV)
>
> ¹³ I am the Alpha and the Omega, the First and the Last, the Beginning and the End.

In Revelation 21:6, God the Father is the one who is doing the talking.

> Revelation 21:6 (NIV)
>
> ⁶ He said to me: "It is done. I am the Alpha and the Omega, the Beginning and the End. To the thirsty I will give water without cost from the spring of the water of life."

God and Jesus both claim the same thing, "I am the Alpha and the Omega, the Beginning and the End." Making Them one God.

> John 1:1–2 (NIV)
>
> ¹ In the beginning was the Word, and the Word was with God, and the Word was God. ² He was with God in the beginning.

With the verses that we have read so far, you can start to see that Jesus is God. From the beginning of creation, Jesus always existed. Jesus is with God. The Jehovah's Witnesses say that the Greek alphabet does not have the letter "a" in its alphabet (this may be true). To prove that Jesus is not God, the Jehovah's Witnesses like to take John 1:1 and say that if there was an "a" in the Greek alphabet, they would have put an "a" between the words was and God in John 1:1. "And the Word was a god." Meaning Jesus was just a man, called a god. When you read this verse in the Greek language, the subject changes in each part of the verse. The beginning is the first subject in the verse, the Word is the second subject, and God is the last subject.

This is how it reads in the Greek: John 1:1, "In the beginning was the Word, and the Word was with God, and God was the Word." *And God was the Word.* This is self-explanatory; no need for an "a" in front of God. God is the subject. It said, "and God was the Word." We know that the Word is Jesus, and the end of John 1:1 says that God was the Word. Therefore, God is Jesus. The verse is only talking about three subjects: the beginning, the Word, and God, not four subjects; the beginning, the Word, God, and a god. At the beginning of creation (Genesis 1:1) was the Word. The Word, who is Jesus, was with God, and God Himself was the Word, who was with God. Even though God and Jesus are two individuals, they are one God. Look at what Jesus said in the following verses.

John 10:30 (KJV)

[30] I and my Father are one.

John 14:8–9 (NIV)

[8] Philip said, "Lord, show us the Father and that will be enough for us."

[9] Jesus answered: "Don't you know me, Philip, even after I have been among you such a long time? Anyone who has seen me has seen the Father. How can you say, 'Show us the Father'?"

Jesus said, "I and the Father are one." There are those who believe when a couple gets married, that this is what Jesus meant. When a couple gets married, they become one. Yes, when a couple gets married, they become one in holy matrimony, but that is not the same as God and Jesus being one. There is no comparison at all. The couple becomes one in marriage, but they still have two different individual spirits, and they do not always agree on everything. They did not become the same spirit and will never become so much as one to be able to say if you see one, you see the other. God and Jesus have always been one God with the same Spirit. God and Jesus always agree on everything. God and Jesus are the same God.

When Jesus said, "I and the Father are one." Jesus meant that He and God are one God. Again, when a couple gets married, they do not become one person or have the same spirit. The married couple are still two individual persons with two different spirits. God is the same one God as God the Father and the same one God as God the Son (Jesus). They are one God. The Jews understood that He was claiming that He is God, and that is why in John 10:33 (KJV), they wanted to stone Him, "33 The Jews answered him, saying, For a good work we stone thee not; but for blasphemy; and because that thou, being a man, makest thyself God."

In John 14:8–9, Jesus makes the exact same claim when He said to Philip, "Anyone who has seen me has seen the Father. How can you say, 'Show us the Father'?" Jesus is saying there is no difference between Him and God the Father because if you know Him, you know the Father; if you've seen Him, you have seen the Father.

In the Bible, both God the Father and God the Son (Jesus) say, "Obey My commandments." Both God and Jesus say, "I am the Alpha and the Omega, the Beginning and the End." With all the evidence of the verses that we read in this chapter, how can anyone say that Jesus is not God or that God is not Jesus? With this evidence I have to say God is Jesus, and Jesus is God. They are two individuals but the same God.

What Jesus is not saying is that God the Father looks like Him. What Jesus is saying is, "I am God the Father; We are one and the same." "I and the Father are one." "Anyone who has seen Me has seen the Father." "Besides being God the Son, I am God the Father." Yes, they are two separate individuals, but they are still the same God. "Mike, what about the Holy Spirit?" I am so glad you asked that question.

Before I answer your question, this is for those who have never read the Bible and those who do not understand the Bible. Whenever you see Spirit capitalized in the Bible without "Holy" in front of it, it is still talking about the Holy Spirit.

John 14:6 (KJV)

⁶ Jesus saith, unto him, I am the way, the truth, and the life: no man cometh unto the Father, but by me.

1 John 5:6 (NIV)

⁶ This is the one who came by water and blood—Jesus Christ. He did not come by water only, but by water and blood. And it is the Spirit who testifies, because the Spirit is the truth.

In 1 John 5:6, I do not want to point out all of what the verse is saying because there is too much to explain. I only want to point out what the last part of the verse is saying. It is saying that the Holy Spirit is the truth. In John 14:6, Jesus said He is the truth. My point is Jesus and the Holy Spirit both are the truth, sharing the same attribute.

Romans 8:9 (KJV)

⁹ But ye are not in the flesh, but in the Spirit, if so be that the Spirit of God dwell in you. Now if any man have not the Spirit of Christ, he is none of his.

There is something to notice in Romans 8:9 besides what is being talked about. In the first half of the verse, the Holy Spirit is the Spirit of God, and in the second half, the Holy Spirit is the Spirit of Christ. The Holy Spirit is the Spirit of God and Jesus; both have the same Spirit.

Matthew 28:19 (NIV)

¹⁹ Therefore go and make disciples of all nations, baptizing them in the name of the Father and of the Son and of the Holy Spirit.

In Matthew 28:19, Jesus is identifying all three of them as having equal power, influence, and authority by saying, "Baptizing them in the name of the Father and of the Son and of the Holy Spirit." Consequently, they are being baptized in God.

1 Corinthians 3:16 (NIV)

¹⁶ "Don't you know that you yourselves are God's temple and that God's Spirit dwells in your midst?"

1 Corinthians 6:19 (NIV)

¹⁹ "Do you not know that your bodies are temples of the Holy Spirit, who is in you, whom you have received from God? You are not your own"

In 1 Corinthians 3:16, we see that our bodies are God's temple and God's Spirit dwells in us. In 1 Corinthians 6:19, we see that our bodies are the Holy Spirit's temple and the Holy Spirit dwells and lives in us. Our bodies are the temple of God and the Holy Spirit. Both of them share the same authority over our bodies. We have the Holy Spirit dwelling in us. God and the Holy Spirit are one God.

1 Corinthians 8:6 (NIV)

⁶ Yet for us there is but one God, the Father, from whom all things came and for whom we live; and there is but one Lord, Jesus Christ, through whom all things came and through whom we live.

Deuteronomy 6:4 (KJV)

⁴ Hear, O Israel: The LORD our God is one LORD.

Second Corinthians 3:17 (NIV)

¹⁷ Now the Lord is the Spirit, and where the Spirit of the Lord is, there is freedom.

Ephesians 4:4–5 (KJV)

⁴ There is one body, and one Spirit, even as ye are called in one hope of your calling; 5 One Lord, one faith, one baptism.

The verses we just read are very clear; they are not complicated or hard to understand. They are straightforward and directly to the point of who the Lord is and that there is only one Lord. There is one Lord, Jesus Christ; the Lord our God is one Lord; and the Lord is the Spirit (Spirit meaning the Holy Spirit). There is one body and one Spirit, one Lord, one faith, one baptism. God is the Lord, Jesus Christ is the Lord, and the Holy Spirit is the Lord, yet there is only one Lord. To summarize, if there is only one Lord and all three of them are Lord, then they are the same Lord, being the same God.

Therefore, with all the evidence in this chapter, God the Father, God the Son (Jesus), and God the Holy Spirit are one God. The three-in-one and the one-in-three. There is one God and He is three individuals. I rest my case.

Side note: The Jehovah's Witnesses, I do not know how, now believe that Jesus Christ was Michael the archangel.

CHAPTER 21:

A Short Review and Closing

This chapter is just a very short summary of what we read and learned.

The Bible does not say you are saved by your baptism. "But Mike, the Bible says in 1 Peter 3:21, 'Baptism doth also now save us.'" Let's finish the verse. "But the answer [the pledge] of a good conscience toward God," meaning your responding to God (being saved) by the resurrection of Jesus Christ. The rest of the verse agrees with Romans 10:9–10. The Bible does actually say if you believe, accept, receive, and confess the Lord Jesus Christ, you will be saved. Clearly, this is not saying that your water baptism saves you.

The Bible does actually say, "Confess your sins one to another" (James 5:16). The Bible does not say that after confessing your sins one to another, then ask the person to go to Jesus and request that He go to God for the forgiveness of your sins in order to get your sins forgiven. The Bible does say to ask Jesus to forgive you of your sins (1 John 2:1). The Bible does not say there is another way to get your sins forgiven.

The Bible does actually say there is one God and one mediator between God and man, the man Christ Jesus (1 Timothy 2:5). "Why did Timothy start by saying there is one God?" One of the reasons is that there is only one God: God the Father, God the Son, and God the Holy Spirit. They are one God. Timothy is pointing out that just as there is only one God, there is only one mediator, Jesus Christ, between God and man. The Bible does not say there are other mediators between Jesus and man.

In 1 John 2:1–2, the Bible does say Jesus is our advocate, the propitiation for our sin. The Bible does not say there are any other mediators or advocates between God and man or between Jesus and man. Nor does the Bible say there are any other mediators, advocates, or propitiations by anyone else at all. The Bible does not tell us to do or believe something about God just because it makes sense. The question is, are your beliefs clearly stated in the Bible without taking verses out of context?

Remember, people who say, "That is just your interpretation of the verses in the Bible," or "It all depends on how you look at it," do not have a full understanding of what they read in the Bible. They definitely did not study the Bible. And they know they cannot disprove what they are being told.

SHORT CLOSING

No religion gave man the Bible, nor did man give man the Bible, but man was inspired by God to write the Bible. God the Holy Spirit told man what to write in the Bible. The Bible does not have contradictions in it because God is not a God of confusion but a God of peace of mind. God the Father, God the Son (Jesus), and God the Holy Spirit love us very, very, very much. You are very important to God. God gave you His Son, Jesus Christ. Jesus Christ loves you so much that He paid a great price for your sins. He saved you from hell and gave you eternal life in heaven. Jesus is our advocate, the atoning sacrifice for our sins. We must be born again by accepting Jesus as our personal Savior.

God wants you to repent and turn away from sin. You are to love God with all your heart. God and Jesus want a strong, loving personal relationship with you. You are first born physically from Mom and Dad. Then, when you receive Jesus Christ as your personal Savior, you are born spiritually by the Holy Spirit. This is called being born again because now your spirit has become alive. Water baptism does not save you. Water baptism and being born again are not the same thing. Being born again is what gets you into heaven by the resurrection of Jesus Christ.

After we receive Jesus Christ as our Savoir, we should get water baptized to testify publicly that we are born again.

Receive Jesus Christ today. Be converted (born again), be a doer of the Word. Do not be a doer of man-made beliefs. Read your Bible so that you know what you are being taught is the truth. You cannot know God's will for you if you do not read the Bible. If what you are being taught about God does not line up with the Bible or you cannot find it in the Bible, then it is not true or of God. The Holy Spirit will help you to understand the Bible. Go to a church that teaches that you must be born again, as taught in the Bible and how I've described it in this book. God wants you to become a true worshiper.

Once again, to help you become a strong Christian, read these books in the Bible in the following order: first, the Gospel of John, then read Galatians, Ephesians, Philippians, and Colossians, and then read 1 and 2 Corinthians. After reading these books, you should be ready to read the books 1 John, Acts, and Romans. After reading these books in the Bible, God, Jesus, and the Holy Spirit will guide you on what to read next. Become the strong Christian that God wants you to become. It is not always easy, but you can do it. Remember God, Jesus, and the Holy Spirit love you very much. They are waiting for you with open arms. God is never too busy for you. The Holy Spirit is with you and in you. The Holy Spirit will help, guide, and encourage you. You are not alone.

Remember, being born again is not a religion or a religious belief. It is not about being religious at all. One can be very religious and still not be born again. Being religious or very religious will not and does not make you born again.

Having a personal relationship with God the Father, God the Son (Jesus Christ), and God the Holy Spirit is what being born again is all about. Faith without good works is dead, but your salvation is based on Jesus Christ; He saved you. Knowing and doing the things that I said in this book will help you to have a strong personal relationship with God, the three-in-one. Let the Bible be your manual and guide in your spiritual life.

There are a lot more verses on the subjects that I talked about in this book, and as you read and study the Bible, you will know them when you come across them. You may think that I could have used some other verses on a subject. I know because I think that way at times when I hear a message. As a study guide, you can use this book to help others to become born again. The Bible should be your main guide in life. I suggest you read all the Bible, not just parts of it.

I feel like I must state the following note because of the things I wrote.

Note: If you are going to leave the church that you are going to and you have been going there for a while and you know the minister, don't just up and leave. Be courteous to your minister. Let your minister know why you are leaving, and try to leave on good terms. Also, make sure you have another church to go to before you leave. Think it over and make sure you are leaving for the right reasons. Make sure this is what God wants you to do. I guess I don't want people to up and leave their church just because of what I have written in this book unless your church does not teach being born again as it is taught in the Bible.

Again, for those who have never read the Bible, the table of contents will tell you where each book is in the Bible. For example, when you see John 3:16, the name John is the book in the Bible, the number before the colon is the chapter, and the number after the colon is the verse in that chapter. The chapter number is usually a little bigger than the verse number in the Bible.

What you have learned in this book is a good beginning, but there still is a lot more to learn about God and Jesus. Smile; life is short here on Earth, and God loves you. May God bless you and be with you always.

CHAPTER 22:

GUIDELINES TO STUDYING THE BIBLE BY PASTOR RUBEN CEBALLOS

- Build a good spiritual database of Bible references and Bible accounts in your heart, soul, and mind by just your general reading of the Bible. Do this randomly as the Holy Spirit leads you.

- Do not try to purposely memorize Bible verses, references, and chapters; just get familiar with the Word, and the Holy Spirit will bring it to your remembrance. It will be there when you need it; trust Him (I call this a spiritual scan).

- Let the Holy Spirit choose a topic or impress one in your heart that is relevant to your current situation or calling, then follow it through in your concordance and cross-references in your Bible.

- Be open as you write down your thoughts to hear what the Holy Spirit is saying and which scriptures He will pull out of your spiritual database that will bring out the revelation and truth He wants you to know and teach.

- Look for and be open to the way He wants you to apply your teaching and notes He gives you.

- Go over your notes at least five times before sharing them, allowing the Holy Spirit to fine-tune and add those personal experiences and examples and ways He wants you to present or go with the topic.

- File your studies away topically in notebooks because the Holy Spirit will add to them later on and birth other studies from them. Remember, it's precept upon precept, line upon line, etc.

- Always remember, the Holy Spirit uses your personality (sanctified) and your life experiences to bring His Word into the natural realm where people can see it and understand it.

- Don't keep the Word in the spirit realm, but bring it from the spirit realm into the natural realm where people can receive it. Be real! Jesus was a master at doing this.

Study Guide and Tools by Pastor Ruben Ceballos

- Read the Proverbs through yearly.
- Try to set a daily routine for your study time without being legalistic or religious about it; you can flex some. This helps you to discipline yourself and also your time. Try not to miss too many days, and be careful of those little detours.
- Good Reference Bible—nothing too complicated or with too much commentary; this tends to distract and sidetrack your hearing from the Holy Spirit.
- Good Bible Dictionary—the best one I have found is the "Liberty Illustrated Bible Dictionary" by Nelson Publishers and Liberty Bible College. It has a great pronunciation tool.
- Good Bible Concordance—a simple and good one is "Cruden's Complete Concordance." I use this 90 percent of the time. The Strong's Concordance is okay for more mature and learned believers. It tends to get people sidetracked too much on word studies (Hebrew and Greek meanings). It's an okay tool for disciplined people.
- Finally, always keep a notebook and pen ready and your ears open. God teaches you not only through His Word but through your daily walk of Faith.

Through people, situations, circumstances, nature, etc. We learn vital lessons on how to apply His eternal, unchanging Word.

What Jesus Is from Genesis to Revelation by Pastor Ruben Ceballos

OLD TESTAMENT

Genesis—Seed of Abraham.

Exodus—The Great I Am.

Leviticus—Peace Offering, Sweet Smelling Savior.

Numbers—The Start Out of Jacob.

Deuteronomy—Rock of Salvation.

Joshua—Captain of the Lord of Host.

Judges—Gideon's Sword of the Lord.

Ruth—Kinsman Redemption.

1 Samuel—Strength of Israel.

2 Samuel—The Rock of Israel.

1 Kings—The Glory Cloud, Elijah's God of Fire.

2 Kings—Elisha's Double Portion, Elijah's Mantle.

1 Chronicles—God's Anointed.

2 Chronicles—Restorer of God's Temple.

Ezra—Nail in His Holy Place.

Nehemiah—Rebuilder of God's City and Restorer of Worship.

Esther—The Deliverer of God's People.

Job—Days Man.

Psalm—The Anointed, the Good Shepherd.

Proverbs—Wisdom of God.

Ecclesiastes—The Preacher.

Song of Solomon—Sweetest Rose of Sharon.

Isaiah—Wonderful, Counselor, Mighty God.

Jeremiah—The Lord Our Righteousness.

Lamentations—Weeping Prophet.

Ezekiel—Wheel in the Middle of the Wheel.

Daniel—Ancient of Days, the Fourth Man in the Furnace.

Hosea—Maker of Israel, the Dew unto Israel, The Healer of the Backslider.

Joel—Former Rain and Latter Rain.

Amos—Tabernacle of David.

Obadiah—House of Jacob.

Jonah—Salvation of the Lord.

Micah—Tower of the Rock.

Nahum—Holiness, Vengeance Judge.

Habakkuk—The Strength of God.

Zephaniah—King of Israel.

Haggai—The Desire of All Nations.

Zechariah—The Branch.

Malachi—Son of Righteousness, Rise with Healing in His Wings.

NEW TESTAMENT

Matthew—Emmanuel, God with Us, King of the Jews, the Son of God, Great Physician, the Friend of Sinners, Savior of the Seed.

Mark—Holy One of God, Son of the Blessed.

Luke—Son of the Highest, Horn of Salvation, Dayspring, Savior.

John—The Word, Bread from Heaven, Bread of Life, Creator, Door, I Am, Only-Begotten, Resurrection and the Life, the Way, the Truth, and the Life.

Acts—Holy one of God, Baptizer with the Holy Spirit, Prince of Life, Holy Child, Just One, Judge of the Quick and the Dead.

Romans—Deliverer, Righteousness of God.

1 Corinthians—Lord of Glory, Foundation, Passover, Last Adam, the Power of God.

2 Corinthians—Image of God, Unspeakable Gift.

Galatians—Seed of Abraham, Redeemer from the Curse, Our Liberty.

Ephesians—Beloved, Chief Cornerstone, the Giver of Gifts, Our Joint Heir, the Breastplate of Righteousness.

Philippians—The Name Which Is above Every Name, Peace That Passes All Understanding, our Strengthener, the Supplier of All Our Needs.

Colossians—Head of the Church, Firstborn from the Dead, Fullness of the Godhead, our Completeness, Image of the Invisible God.

1 Thessalonians—Blessed Hope, the Rapture of the Church.

2 Thessalonians—The Soon-Coming King to Execute Vengeance on the Wicked.

1 Timothy—King of the Ages, God in the flesh, Mediator, King of Kings, Ransom for All.

2 Timothy—Seed of David.

Titus—Lord Christ Our Savior.

Philemon—Our Fellowship.

Hebrews—Brightness of His Glory, Upholder of All Things, Captain of Salvation, Apostle and High Priest, Forerunner, Great High Priest, Minister of the Sanctuary, Author and Finisher of Our Faith, Great Shepherd of the Sheep.

James—The Lawgiver, the Name of the Lord.

1 Peter—Chief Cornerstone, Bishop of Our Souls, Chief Shepherd.

2 Peter—Daystar, Day dawn.

1 John—Advocate, Cleanser of All Sin, Jesus Christ the Righteous, Eternal Life.

2 John—Son of the Father.

3 John—The Will of God to Prosper and Be in Health Even as Our Soul Prosper.

Jude—Builder of Our Holy Faith and Keeper of Our Love in God.

Revelation—Faithful Witness, Prince of the Kings of the Earth, Alpha and Omega, the Beginning and the Ending, the First and the Last, Morning Star, the Amen, Faithful and True Witness, Beginning of Creation, Lion of the Tribe of Judah, the Root of David, the Word of God, Bright and Morning Star, King of Kings and Lord of Lords, the One That Said Behold I Come Quickly.

EVEN SO, COME LORD JESUS!

When Were the Books of the Bible Written?

OLD TESTAMENT

Job—Unknown

Genesis—1445–1405 BC

Exodus—1445–1405 BC

Leviticus—1445–1405 BC

Numbers—1445–1405 BC

Deuteronomy—1445–1405 BC

Psalms—1410–450 BC

Joshua—1405–1385 BC

Judges—ca. 1043 BC

Ruth—ca. 1030–1010 BC

Song of Solomon—971–965 BC

Proverbs—ca. 971–686 BC

Ecclesiastes—940–931 BC

1 Samuel—931–722 BC

2 Samuel—931–722 BC

Obadiah—850–840 BC

Joel—835–796 BC

Jonah—ca. 775 BC

Amos—ca. 750 BC

Hosea—750–710 BC

Micah—735–710 BC

Isaiah—700–681 BC

Nahum—ca. 650 BC

Zephaniah—635–625 BC

Habakkuk—615–605 BC

Ezekiel—590–570 BC

Lamentations—586 BC

Jeremiah—586–570 BC

1 Kings—561–538 BC

2 Kings—561–538 BC

Daniel—536–530 BC

Haggai—ca. 520 BC

Zechariah—480–470 BC

Ezra—457–444 BC

1 Chronicles—450–430 BC

2 Chronicles—450–430 BC

Esther—450–331 BC

Malachi—433–424 BC

Nehemiah—424–400 BC

NEW TESTAMENT

James—AD 44–49

Galatians—AD 49–50

Matthew—AD 50—60.

Mark—AD 50–60

1 Thessalonians—AD 51

2 Thessalonians—AD 51–52

1 Corinthians—AD 55

2 Corinthians—AD 55–56

Romans—AD 56

Luke—AD 60–61

Ephesians—AD 60–62

Philippians—AD 60–62

Philemon—AD 60–62

Colossians—AD 60–62

Acts—AD 62

1 Timothy—AD 62–64

Titus—AD 62–64

1 Peter—AD 64–65

2 Timothy—AD 66–67

2 Peter—AD 67–68

Hebrews—AD 67–69

Jude—AD 68–70

John—AD 80–90

1 John—AD 90–95

2 John—AD 90–95

3 John—AD 90–95

Revelation—AD 94–96